THE PEOPLE, YES

BY CARL SANDBURG

ABRAHAM LINCOLN: THE PRAIRIE YEARS

THE AMERICAN SONGBAG

POEMS

SMOKE AND STEEL

SLABS OF THE SUNBURNT WEST

CHICAGO POEMS

CORNHUSKERS

GOOD MORNING, AMERICA

SELECTED POEMS. Edited by Rebecca West

FOR YOUNG FOLKS

ROOTABAGA STORIES

ROOTABAGA PIGEONS

ABE LINCOLN GROWS UP

The People, Yes

Carl Sandburg

HARCOURT, BRACE AND COMPANY

NEW YORK

FIRST EDITION

AFTER PRINTING 270 DE LUXE COPIES

THE DE LUXE EDITION CONSISTS OF 270 COPIES ON WORTHY
PERMANENT BOOK ANTIQUE, NUMBERED AND SIGNED BY THE
AUTHOR, OF WHICH 250 COPIES ARE FOR SALE.

13547

Typography by Robert Josephy

PRINTED IN THE UNITED STATES OF AMERICA
BY QUINN & BODEN COMPANY, INC., RAHWAY, N. J.

Dedicated
to contributors
dead   and   living

THE PEOPLE, YES

*Being several stories and psalms nobody
would want to laugh at*

*interspersed with memoranda variations
worth a second look*

*along with sayings and yarns traveling on
grief and laughter*

*running sometimes as a fugitive air in the
classic manner*

*breaking into jig time and tap dancing
nohow classical*

*and further broken by plain and irregular
sounds and echoes from*

*the roar and whirl of street crowds, work
gangs, sidewalk clamor,*

*with interludes of midnight cool blue and
inviolable stars*

over the phantom frames of skyscrapers.

THE PEOPLE, YES

I

From the four corners of the earth,
from corners lashed in wind
and bitten with rain and fire,
from places where the winds begin
and fogs are born with mist children,
tall men from tall rocky slopes came
and sleepy men from sleepy valleys,
their women tall, their women sleepy,
with bundles and belongings,
with little ones babbling, "Where to now?
    what next?"

The people of the earth, the family of man,
wanted to put up something proud to look at,
a tower from the flat land of earth
on up through the ceiling into the top of the sky.

And the big job got going,
the caissons and pilings sunk,
floors, walls and winding staircases
aimed at the stars high over,
aimed to go beyond the ladders of the moon.

And God Almighty could have struck them dead
or smitten them deaf and dumb.

And God was a whimsical fixer.
God was an understanding Boss
with another plan in mind,

And suddenly shuffled all the languages,
    changed the tongues of men
    so they all talked different
And the masons couldn't get what the hodcarriers said,
The helpers handed the carpenters the wrong tools,
Five hundred ways to say, "W h o a r e y o u ?"
Changed ways of asking, "Where do we go from here?"
Or of saying, "Being born is only the beginning,"
Or, "Would you just as soon sing as make that noise?"
Or, "What you don't know won't hurt you."
And the material-and-supply men started disputes
With the hauling gangs and the building trades
And the architects tore their hair over the blueprints
And the brickmakers and the mule skinners talked back
To the straw bosses who talked back to the superintendents
And the signals got mixed; the men who shovelled the bucket
Hooted the hoisting men—and the job was wrecked.

Some called it the Tower of Babel job
And the people gave it many other names.
The wreck of it stood as a skull and a ghost,
a memorandum hardly begun,
swaying and sagging in tall hostile winds,
held up by slow friendly winds.

From Illinois and Indiana came a later myth
Of all the people in the world at Howdeehow
For the first time standing together:
From six continents, seven seas, and several archipelagoes,
From points of land moved by wind and water
Out of where they used to be to where they are,
The people of the earth marched and travelled
To gather on a great plain.

At a given signal they would join in a shout,
    So it was planned,
One grand hosannah, something worth listening to.
    And they all listened.
    The signal was given.
    And they all listened.
    And the silence was beyond words.
They had come to listen, not to make a noise.
    They wanted to hear.
So they all stood still and listened,
Everybody except a little old woman from Kalamazoo
Who gave out a long slow wail over what she was missing
    because she was stone deaf.

This is the tale of the Howdeehow powpow,
One of a thousand drolls the people tell of themselves,
Of tall corn, of wide rivers, of big snakes,
Of giants and dwarfs, heroes and clowns,
Grown in the soil of the mass of the people.

3

In the long flat panhandle of Texas
far off on the grassland of the cattle country
near noon they sight a rider coming toward them
and the sky may be a cold neverchanging gray
or the sky may be changing its numbers
back and forth all day even and odd numbers
and the afternoon slides away somewhere
and they see their rider is alive yet
their rider is coming nearer yet
and they expect what happens and it happens again
he and his horse ride in late for supper
yet not too late
and night is on and the stars are out
and night too slides away somewhere
night too has even and odd numbers.

The wind brings "a norther"
to the long flat panhandle
and in the shivering cold they say:
  "Between Amarilla and the North Pole
    is only a barb wire fence,"
which they give a twist:
  "Out here the only windbreak
    is the North Star."

4

The people know what the land knows
the numbers odd and even of the land
the slow hot wind of summer and its withering
or again the crimp of the driving white blizzard
and neither of them to be stopped
neither saying anything else than:
> "I'm not arguing. I'm telling you."

The old-timer on the desert was gray
and grizzled with ever seeing the sun:
> "For myself I don't care whether it rains.
> I've seen it rain.
> But I'd like to have it rain
> pretty soon sometime.
> Then my son could see it.
> He's never seen it rain."

"Out here on the desert,"
> said the first woman who said it,
>> "the first year you don't believe
>> what others tell you
>> and the second year you don't
>> believe what you tell yourself."

"I weave thee, I weave thee,"
> sang the weaving Sonora woman.
"I weave thee,
> thou art for a Sonora fool."

And the fool spoke of her,
over wine mentioned her:
"She can teach a pair of stilts to dance."

"What is the east? Have you been in the east?"
the New Jersey woman asked the little girl
the wee child growing up in Arizona who said:
"Yes, I've been in the east,
  the east is where trees come
  between you and the sky."

Another baby in Cleveland, Ohio,
in Cuyahoga County, Ohio—
why did she ask:
                    "Papa,
                    what is the moon
                    supposed to advertise?"

And the boy in Winnetka, Illinois who wanted to know:
"Is there a train so long you can't count the cars?
  Is there a blackboard so long it will hold all the numbers?"

What of the Athenian last year on whose bosom
a committee hung a medal to say to the world
here is a champion heavyweight poet?
He stood on a two-masted schooner
and flung his medal far out on the sea bosom.
    "And why not?
    Has anybody ever given the ocean a medal?
    Who of the poets equals the music of the sea?

8

And where is a symbol of the people
                              unless it is the sea?"
"Is it far to the next town?"
asked the Arkansas traveller
who was given the comfort:
        "It seems farther than it is
        but you'll find it ain't."

Six feet six was Davy Tipton
and he had the proportions
as kingpin Mississippi River pilot
nearly filling the pilothouse
as he took the wheel with a laugh:
"Big rivers ought to have big men."

On the homestretch of a racetrack
in the heart of the bluegrass country
in Lexington, Kentucky
they strewed the ashes of a man
who had so ordered in his will.
        He loved horses
        and wanted his dust
in the flying hoofs of the homestretch.

5

For sixty years the pine lumber barn
had held cows, horses, hay, harness, tools, junk,
amid the prairie winds of Knox County, Illinois
and the corn crops came and went, plows and wagons,
and hands milked, hands husked and harnessed
and held the leather reins of horse teams
in dust and dog days, in late fall sleet
till the work was done that fall.
And the barn was a witness, stood and saw it all.
 "That old barn on your place, Charlie,
  was nearly falling last time I saw it,
  how is it now?"
 "I got some poles to hold it on the east side
  and the wind holds it up on the west."

6

And you take hold of a handle
　　by one hand or the other
　　by the better or worse hand
　　and you never know
　　maybe till long afterward
　　which was the better hand.

　　And you give an anecdote
out of profound and moving forms of life
and one says you're an odd bird to tell it
and it was whimsical entertaining thank you
while another takes it as a valentine
　　and a fable not solved offhand
　　a text for two hours talk and
　　　　several cigars smoked—
You might say there never was a man who cut
　　off his nose to spite his face.
Yet the cartoon stands for several nations
　　and more than one ruler of a realm.
Likewise the man who burned his barn to get
　　rid of the rats
Or the woman who said her "No" meant "Perhaps"
　　and her "Perhaps" meant "Yes"
Or Monte Cristo yes he was a case.

Monte Cristo had a list, a little roll call.
And one by one he took them each for a ride
Saying One and Two and Three and so on

Till the names were all crossed off
And he had cleansed the world of a given number
Of betrayers who had personally wronged him.
He was judge, jury, and executioner,
On a par with Frankie who shot Johnnie,
Only far colder than Frankie.
        "He created a solitude
        and called it peace."
He was cold, sure, and what they call elevated,
Meaning it was justice and not personal malice
Handing out stiff death with regards, compliments,
Calling each number like Nemesis in knickerbockers.
        The show he put on was a little too good.
        He was a lone wolf all on his own.
        And Jesse James beat his record.
And John Brown was a far more profound sketch,
John Brown who was locked up and didn't stay locked,
John Brown who was buried deep and didn't stay so.

        In a Colorado graveyard
        two men lie in one grave.
They shot it out in a jam over who owned
One corner lot: over a piece of real estate
They shot it out: it was a perfect duel.
Each cleansed the world of the other.
Each horizontal in an identical grave
Had his bones cleaned by the same maggots.
They sleep now as two accommodating neighbors.
They had speed and no control.
They wanted to go and didn't know where.

"Revenge takes time and is a lot of bother,"
   said a released convict who by the code
   of Monte Cristo should have shot twelve
   jurymen and hanged one judge and cruci-
   fied one prosecuting attorney and hung by
   thumbs two police officers and four prom-
   inent citizens.
"In my case," he added, "it pays to have a
   good forgettery."

7

Neither wife nor child had Mr. Eastman and the manner of his
death was peculiar.

Around a fireplace in his home one night he entertained eight old
friends, saying to one woman at the door at eleven o'clock,
"I'm leaving you," she rejoining, "No, I'm leaving you."

But Mr. Eastman, the kodak king of exactly how many millions
he wasn't sure, knew better as to whether he was leaving her
or she him.

After a good night of sleep and breakfast he met two lawyers and
a secretary, rearranging codicils in his will

And when they lingered and delayed about going, he said, "You
must be going, I have some writing to do,"

And they had a feeling, "Well, this is one of Mr. Eastman's jokes,
he has always had his odd pleasantries."

And again Mr. Eastman knew better than they that there was a
little writing to be done and nobody else could do it for him.

They went—and Mr. Eastman stepped into a bathroom, took his
reliable fountain pen and scribbled on a sheet of paper:

"My work is finished. Why wait?"

He had counted the years one by one up to seventy-seven, had
come through one paralytic stroke, had seen one lifelong
friend reduced by a series of strokes to childish play at
papercutting four years in bed and the integrity of the mind
gone.

He had a guess deep in his heart that if he lived he might change
his will; he could name cases; as the will now stood it was a
keen dispersal for science, music, research, and with a changing mind he might change his will.

Cool he was about what he was doing for he had thought about
it along the slopes of the Genesee Valley of New York and
along the coasts of Africa and amid babbling apes of the
jungle.

He inspects in the bath-room an automatic revolver, a weapon
tested and trusted, loaded, oiled, operating.
He takes a towel and wets it, placing it over the heart, the idea
being that in case he shoots himself there will be no soot nor
splatter and a clean piece of workmanship.
His preparations are considered and thorough and he knows the
credit for the deed can never possibly go to anyone but himself.
Then he steps out, the hammer falls, he crosses over, takes the
last barrier.
He knows thereafter no console organist will call of a morning
to play Bach or Handel while he eats breakfast.
His last testament stands secure against the childishness of second
childhood.

8

Mildred Klinghofer whirled through youth in bloom.
One baby came and was taken away, another came and was taken
　　away.
From her windows she saw the cornrows young and green
And later the final stand of the corn and the huddled shocks
And the blue mist of a winter thaw deepening at evening.
In her middle forties her first husband died.
In her middle sixties her second husband died.
In her middle seventies her third husband died.
And she died at mid-eighty with her fourth husband at the bed-
　　side.
Thus she had known an editor, a lawyer, a grocer, a retired
　　farmer.
To the first of them she had borne two children she had hun-
　　gered for.
And deep in her had stayed a child hunger.
In the last hours when her mind wandered, she cried imperiously,
　　"My baby! give me my baby!"
And her cries for this child, born of her mind, in her final mo-
　　ments of life, went on and on.
When they answered, "Your baby isn't here" or "Your baby is
　　coming soon if you will wait," she kept on with her cry,
　　"My baby! let me hold my baby!"
　　　　And they made a rag doll
　　　　And laid it in her arms
And she clutched it as a mother would.
And she was satisfied and her second childhood ended like her
　　first, with a doll in her arms.

There are dreams stronger than death.

Men and women die holding these dreams.

Yes, "stronger than death": let the hammers beat on this slogan.

Let the sea wash its salt against it and the blizzards drive wind and winter at it.

Let the undersea sharks try to break this bronze murmur.

Let the gentle bush dig its root deep and spread upward to split one boulder.

Blame the frustrate? Some of them have lived stronger than death.

Blame only the smug and scrupulous beyond reproach.

Who made the guess Shakespeare died saying his best plays didn't get written?

Who swindles himself more deeply than the one saying, "I am holier than thou"?

> "I love you,"
>   said a great mother.
> "I love you for what you are
>   knowing so well what you are.
>   And I love you more yet, child,
>   deeper yet than ever, child,
>   for what you are going to be,
>   knowing so well you are going far,
>   knowing your great works are ahead,
>   ahead and beyond,
>   yonder and far over yet."

9

A father sees a son nearing manhood.
What shall he tell that son?
"Life is hard; be steel; be a rock."
And this might stand him for the storms
and serve him for humdrum and monotony
and guide him amid sudden betrayals
and tighten him for slack moments.
"Life is a soft loam; be gentle; go easy."
And this too might serve him.
Brutes have been gentled where lashes failed.
The growth of a frail flower in a path up
has sometimes shattered and split a rock.
A tough will counts. So does desire.
So does a rich soft wanting.
Without rich wanting nothing arrives.
Tell him too much money has killed men
and left them dead years before burial:
the quest of lucre beyond a few easy needs
has twisted good enough men
sometimes into dry thwarted worms.
Tell him time as a stuff can be wasted.
Tell him to be a fool every so often
and to have no shame over having been a fool
yet learning something out of every folly
hoping to repeat none of the cheap follies
thus arriving at intimate understanding
of a world numbering many fools.
Tell him to be alone often and get at himself

and above all tell himself no lies about himself
whatever the white lies and protective fronts
he may use amongst other people.
Tell him solitude is creative if he is strong
and the final decisions are made in silent rooms.
Tell him to be different from other people
if it comes natural and easy being different.
Let him have lazy days seeking his deeper motives.
Let him seek deep for where he is a born natural.
        Then he may understand Shakespeare
        and the Wright brothers, Pasteur, Pavlov,
        Michael Faraday and free imaginations
bringing changes into a world resenting change.
        He will be lonely enough
        to have time for the work
        he knows as his own.

The Australian mounted infantryman now teaches
    in a western state college.
Once he studied at the University of Heidelberg
    and took a doctor's degree.
Once he slept on newspapers, pink sheets, three
    weeks in Grant Park, Chicago
Keeping a tight hold on his certificate awarded
    by the University of Heidelberg.
Once he lived six weeks in a tent looking in the
    face the Great Sphinx of Egypt.
Once of a morning shaving he happened to ask the
    battered and worndown Sphinx,
"What would you say if I should ask you to tell
    me something worth telling?"
And the Sphinx broke its long silence:
                    "Don't expect too much."

II

An Englishman in the old days
presented the Empress of Russia
with a life-sized flea made of gold
and it could hop.

She asked the court:
"What can we Russians do
 to equal this marvel?"

A Minister took it away
and brought it back soon after.
He had seen to it
and had the monogram of the Empress
engraved on each foot of the flea
though it would no longer hop.

This is a case in point
as told by Salzman
who came from the Caucasus
and had it from a man who was there.

In Tiflis, his home town,
Salzman knew a merchant
who stood in the front door
and spoke to passersby,
to possible customers:
     "Come inside.
      We've got everything—
      even bird's milk."

And this merchant weighed his hand
along with what he sold his patrons
and each evening after business hours
he threw holy water on his hand
saying, "Cleanse thyself, cleanse thyself."

Among the peasants Salzman heard:
"He should be the owner of the land
    who rubs it between his hands every spring."

Wood rangers in the forest of the czar
came in and talked all night.
They spoke of forest sounds:
"The cry of a virgin tree at its first cut
        of the ax stays in the air.
"The sound of the blow that kills a snake
        is in the air till sundown.
"The cry of the child wrongfully punished
        stays in the air."

    And this was in the old days
    and they are a fine smoke
    a thin smoke.

    The people move
    in a fine thin smoke,
    the people, yes.

12

The scaffolding holds the arch in place
till the keystone is put in to stay.
Then the scaffolding comes out.
Then the arch stands strong as all the
massed pressing parts of the arch
and loose as any sag or spread
failing of the builders' intention, hope.
    "The arch never sleeps."
    Living in union it holds.
So long as each piece does its work
the arch is alive, singing, a restless choral.

13

The oatstraw green turns gold turns ashen and
    prepares for snow.
The earth and the grass hold grand international
    confabulations with the sun.
Along the Arkansas or the Po grass testifies to
    loam of earth alive yet.
The rivers of the earth run into the sea, return
    in fog and rain alive yet.
The shuttlings go on between field and sky and
    keep corn potatoes beans alive yet.
The Illinois corn leaves spoken to in high winds
    run in sea waves of sun silver.
Alive yet the spillover of last night's moonrise
    brought returns of peculiar cash
    a cash of thin air alive yet.

On the shores of Lake Michigan
high on a wooden pole, in a box,
two purple martins had a home
and taken away down to Martinique
and let loose, they flew home,
thousands of miles to be home again.
    And this has lights of wonder
    echo and pace and echo again.
The birds let out began flying
north north-by-west north
till they were back home.
How their instruments told them

of ceiling, temperature, air pressure,
how their control-boards gave them
reports of fuel, ignition, speeds,
is out of the record, out.

Across spaces of sun and cloud,
in rain and fog, through air pockets,
wind with them, wind against them,
stopping for subsistence rations,
whirling in gust and spiral,
these people of the air,
these children of the wind,
had a sense of where to go and how,
how to go north north-by-west north,
till they came to one wooden pole,
till they were home again.

And this has lights of wonder
echo and pace and echo again
for other children, other people, yes.

The red ball of the sun in an evening mist
Or the slow fall of rain on planted fields
Or the pink sheath of a newborn child
Or the path of a child's mouth to a nipple
Or the snuggle of a bearcub in mother paws
Or the structural weave of the universe
Witnessed in a moving frame of winter stars—
These hold affidavits of struggle.

14

The people is Everyman, everybody.
Everybody is you and me and all others.
What everybody says is what we all say.
        And what is it we all say?

Where did we get these languages?
Why is your baby-talk deep in your blood?
What is the cling of the tongue
To what it heard with its mother-milk?

They cross on the ether now.
They travel on high frequencies
Over the border-lines and barriers
Of mountain ranges and oceans.
When shall we all speak the same language?
And do we want to have all the same language?
Are we learning a few great signs and passwords?
Why should Everyman be lost for words?
The questions are put every day in every tongue:
        "Where you from, Stranger?
        Where were you born?
        Got any money?
        What do you work at?
        Where's your passport?
        Who are your people?"

Over the ether crash the languages.
        And the people listen.

As on the plain of Howdeehow they listen.
    They want to hear.
They will be told when the next war is ready.
The long wars and the short wars will come on the air,
How many got killed and how the war ended
And who got what and the price paid
And how there were tombs for the Unknown Soldier,
    The boy nobody knows the name of,
The boy whose great fame is that of the masses,
The millions of names too many to write on a tomb,
The heroes, the cannonfodder, the living targets,
The mutilated and sacred dead,
The people, yes.

Two countries with two flags
are nevertheless one land, one blood, one people—
    can this be so?
And the earth belongs to the family of man?
    can this be so?

The first world war came and its cost was laid on the people.
The second world war—the third—what will be the cost?
And will it repay the people for what they pay?

From the people the countries get their armies.
By the people the armies are fed, clothed, armed.
Out of the smoke and ashes of the war
The people build again their two countries with two flags
Even though sometimes it is one land, one blood, one people.

Hate is a vapor fixed and mixed.
Hate is a vapor blown and thrown.
And the war lasts till the hate dies down
And the crazy Four Horsemen have handed the people
Hunger and filth and a stink too heavy to stand.
Then the earth sends forth bright new grass
And the land begins to breathe easy again
Though the hate of the people dies slow and hard.
　　　Hate is a lingering heavy swamp mist.

And the bloated horse carcass points four feet to the sky
And the tanks and caterpillar tractors are buried deep in shell
　　holes
And rust flakes the big guns and time rots the gas masks on skele-
　　ton faces:
Deep in the dirt the dynamite threw them with an impersonal
　　detonation: war is "Oh!" and "Ah!": war is "Ugh!"

　　　　　And after the strife of war
　　　　　begins the strife of peace.

16

Hope is a tattered flag and a dream out of time.
Hope is a heartspun word, the rainbow, the shadblow in
    white,
The evening star inviolable over the coal mines,
The shimmer of northern lights across a bitter winter night,
The blue hills beyond the smoke of the steel works,
The birds who go on singing to their mates in peace, war,
    peace,
The ten-cent crocus bulb blooming in a used-car salesroom,
The horseshoe over the door, the luckpiece in the pocket,
The kiss and the comforting laugh and resolve—
Hope is an echo, hope ties itself yonder, yonder.

The spring grass showing itself where least expected,
The rolling fluff of white clouds on a changeable sky,
The broadcast of strings from Japan, bells from Moscow,
Of the voice of the prime minister of Sweden carried
Across the sea in behalf of a world family of nations
And children singing chorals of the Christ child
And Bach being broadcast from Bethlehem, Pennsylvania
And tall skyscrapers practically empty of tenants
And the hands of strong men groping for handholds
And the Salvation Army singing God loves us. . . .

"The people is a myth, an abstraction."
And what myth would you put in place
     of the people?
And what abstraction would you exchange
     for this one?
And when has creative man not toiled
     deep in myth?
And who fights for a bellyful only and
     where is any name worth remembering
     for anything else than the human ab-
     straction woven through it with in-
     visible thongs?
"Precisely who and what is the people?"
Is this far off from asking what is grass?
     what is salt? what is the sea? what is
     loam?
What are seeds? what is a crop? why must
     mammals have milk soon as born or they
     perish?
And how did that alfalfaland governor
     mean it: "The common people is a mule
     that will do anything you say except
     stay hitched"?

Let the nickels and dimes explain.
They are made for the people.
Millions every day study the buffalo on the nickel,
Study the torch of liberty on the dime
And the words "In God We Trust,"
Study before spending the nickel, the dime,
For a handkerchief, a mousetrap, a bowl of soup.

    These with their nickels and dimes
    Bring the street its roar and whirl,
    These in their wants and spending,
These are the bottom pedestals of steel-ribbed skyscrapers.
These are the buyers and payers whose mass flood of nickels
    and dimes is a life stream of a system.

And how come the hey-you-
    -listen-to-this billboard, the you-can't-
    -get-away-from-this electric sign, the
    show window robots and dummies, the loud-
    speaker clamor, the bargains brandished
    with slambang hoots and yells, nods and
    winks, gee-whizz sales?
The liar in print who first lies to you
    about your health and then lies about
    what will fix it, the scare liar who hopes
    his lies will scare you into buying what
    he is lying about,
The better-than-all-others liar, the easy-pay-
    ments liar, the greatest-on-earth liar, the
    get-rich-quick liar

Befouling words and mutilating language and
    feeding rubbish and filth to the human mind
    for the sake of sales, selling whatever can
    be sold for a profit—
Out of this seething whirl, this merciless fight
    of the selling game, what happens to buyers
    and sellers? why does the question rise:
        "How can you compete with a skunk?"

The endless lines of women buying steel-wool dishrags are among
    the people, the customers, the mass buyers who pay
For the barons and counts the American girl goes shopping for,
    trying one and another.
"What is doing in dukes today and how much for a marquis a
    markee?" asks the chain store princess, the daughter of the
    railroad reorganization looter,
While the shoppers and commuters who constitute their meal
    tickets pick the aisles amid frying pans, flannelette apparel,
    leatherette notions, genuine toys and imitation jewelry.

Out of the needs of life and the wants of the people rises a jungle
    of tall possessions bewildering to its owners and their sons
    and daughters who step in when the will is read and say,
    "Now it's ours."
From then on the bank and its branches appurtenant thereto, the
    mills and mines, the patents, the oil wells and pipe lines, the
    monopoly rights, the coast-to-coast chain of stores, belong
    to the new generation,
To a daughter sometimes nothing special, just another cutie; to a
    son who knows neckties and chorines and wisecracks at part-
    ing, "Abyssinia."

Out of this rigamarole come czars of definite domains, owners of control saying, "We don't have to own it. What's ownership anyhow if we hold control and the affiliates and subsidiaries of the main holding company are fixed our way?"

19

The people, yes, the people,
Everyone who got a letter today
And those the mail-carrier missed,
The women at the cookstoves preparing meals,
in a sewing corner mending, in a basement
laundering, woman the homemaker,
The women at the factory tending a stitching
machine, some of them the mainstay of the
jobless man at home cooking, laundering,
Streetwalking jobhunters, walkers alive and keen,
sleepwalkers drifting along, the stupefied and
hopeless down-and-outs, the game fighters
who will die fighting,
Walkers reading signs and stopping to study
windows, the signs and windows aimed
straight at their eyes, their wants,
Women in and out of doors to look and feel, to
try on, to buy and take away, to order and
have it charged and delivered, to pass by on
account of price and conditions,
The shopping crowds, the newspaper circulation,
the bystanders who witness parades, who
meet the boat, the train, who throng in
wavelines to a fire, an explosion, an accident—
The people, yes—
Their shoe soles wearing holes in stone steps, their
hands and gloves wearing soft niches in ban-

34

isters of granite, two worn foot-tracks at the general-delivery window,

Driving their cars, stop and go, red light, green light, and the law of the traffic cop's fingers, on their way, loans and mortgages, margins to cover,

Payments on the car, the bungalow, the radio, the electric icebox, accumulated interest on loans for past payments, the writhing point of where the money will come from,

Crime thrown in their eyes from every angle, crimes against property and person, crime in the prints and films, crime as a lurking shadow ready to spring into reality, crime as a method and a technic,

Comedy as an offset to crime, the laughmakers, the odd numbers in the news and the movies, original clowns and imitators, and in the best you never know what's coming next even when it's hokum,

And sports, how a muff in the seventh lost yesterday's game and now they are learning to hit Dazzy's fadeaway ball and did you hear how Foozly plowed through that line for a touchdown this afternoon?

And daily the death toll of the speed wagons; a cripple a minute in fenders, wheels, steel and glass splinters; a stammering witness before a coroner's jury, "It happened so sudden I don't know what happened."

And in the air a decree: life is a gamble; take a
     chance; you pick a number and see what you
     get: anything can happen in this sweepstakes:
     around the corner may be prosperity or the
     worst depression yet: who knows? nobody:
     you pick a number, you draw a card, you
     shoot the bones.
In the poolrooms the young hear, "Ashes to
     ashes, dust to dust, If the women don't get
     you then the whiskey must," and in the
     churches, "We walk by faith and not by sight,"
Often among themselves in their sessions of can-
     dor the young saying, "Everything's a racket,
     only the gyp artists get by."
And over and beyond the latest crime or comedy
     always that relentless meal ticket saying
     dont-lose-me, hold your job, glue your mind
     on that job or when your last nickel is gone
     you live on your folks or sign for relief,
And the terror of these unknowns is a circle of
     black ghosts holding men and women in toil
     and danger, and sometimes shame, beyond
     the dreams of their blossom days, the days
     before they set out on their own.
What is this "occupational disease" we hear
     about? It's a sickness that breaks your health
     on account of the work you're in. That's all.
     Another kind of work and you'd have been
     as good as any of them. You'd have been
     your old self.

And what is this "hazardous occupation"? Why
that's where you're liable to break your neck
or get smashed on the job so you're no good
on that job any more and that's why you
can't get any regular life insurance so long as
you're on that job.

These are heroes then—among the plain people—
Heroes, did you say? And why not? They
give all they've got and ask no questions and
take what comes and what more do you
want?

On the street you can see them any time, some
with jobs, some nothing doing, here a down-
and-out, there a game fighter who will die
fighting.

20

Who shall speak for the people?
Who knows the works from A to Z
    so he can say, "I know what the
    people want"? Who is this phenom?
    where did he come from?
When have the people been half as rotten
    as what the panderers to the people
    dangle before crowds?
When has the fiber of the people been as
    shoddy as what is sold to the people
    by cheaters?
What is it the panderers and cheaters of
    the people play with and trade on?
The credulity of believers and hopers—and
    when is a heart less of a heart because
    of belief and hope?
What is the tremulous line between credu-
    lity on the one side and on the other
    the hypotheses and illusions of inven-
    tors, discoverers, navigators who chart
    their course by what they hope and
    believe is beyond the horizon?
What is a stratosphere fourteen miles from
    the earth or a sunken glass house on
    the sea-bottom amid fish and feather-
    stars unless a bet that man can shove
    on beyond yesterday's record of man
    the hoper, the believer?

How like a sublime sanctuary of human
credulity is that room where amid
tubes, globes and retorts they shoot
with heavy hearts of hydrogen and
batter with fire-streams of power hoping to smash the atom:
Who are these bipeds trying to take apart
the atom and isolate its electrons and
make it tell why it is what it is? Believers and hopers.
Let the work of their fathers and elder-
brothers be cancelled this instant and
what would happen?
Nothing—only every tool, bus, car, light,
torch, bulb, print, film, instrument or
communication depending for its life
on electrodynamic power would stop
and stand dumb and silent.

Who knows the people, the migratory harvest hands and berry pickers, the loan shark victims, the installment house wolves,

The jugglers in sand and wood who smooth their hands along the mold that casts the frame of your motor-car engine,

The metal polishers, solderers, and paint spray hands who put the final finish on the car,

The riveters and bolt-catchers, the cowboys of the air in the big city, the cowhands of the Great Plains, the ex-convicts, the bellhops, redcaps, lavatory men—

The union organizer with his list of those ready to join and those hesitating, the secret paid informers who report every move toward organizing,

The house-to-house canvassers, the doorbell ringers, the good-morning-have-you-heard boys, the strike pickets, the strike-breakers, the hired sluggers, the ambulance crew, the ambu-lance chasers, the picture chasers, the meter readers, the oysterboat crews, the harborlight tenders—

who knows the people?

Who knows this from pit to peak? The people, yes.

22

The people is a lighted believer and
    hoper—and this is to be held against
    them?
The panderers and cheaters are to have
    their way in trading on these lights
    of the people?
Not always, no, not always, for the people
    is a knower too.
With Johannson steel blocks the people
    can measure itself as a knower
Knowing what it knows today with a deeper
    knowing than ever
Knowing in millionths and billionths of
    an inch
Knowing in the mystery of one automatic
    machine expertly shaping for your eyes
    another automatic machine
Knowing in traction, power-shafts, transmis-
    sion, twist drills, grinding, gears—
Knowing in the night air mail, the news-
    reel flicker, the broadcasts from Tokio,
    Shanghai, Bombay and Somaliland—
The people a knower whose knowing
    grows by what it feeds on
The people wanting to know more, wanting.
The birds of the air and the fish of the sea
    leave off where man begins.

"The kindest and gentlest here are the
   murderers," said the penitentiary warden.
"I killed the man because I loved him,"
   said the woman the police took yesterday.
"I had such a good time," said the woman leaving a movie theater
   with tears in her eyes. "It was a swell picture."
"A divorced man goes and marries the same kind of a woman he
   is just rid of," said the lawyer.
"Life is a gigantic fake," read the farewell note of the highschool
   boy who killed himself.
"I pick jurors with nonconvicting faces,"
   said the lawyer who usually cleared his man.
"We earn and we earn and all that we earn goes into the grave,"
   said the basement-dwelling mother who had lost six of her
   eight children from the white plague.
"Don't mourn for me but organize," said the Utah I.W.W. before
   a firing squad executed sentence of death on him, his last
   words running: "Let her go!"
"Look out or you'll be ready for one of these one-man bungalows
   with silver handles," laughed the traffic cop.
"Tie your hat to the saddle and let's ride,"
   yelled one in a five-gallon hat in Albuquerque.
"If I never see you again don't think the time long," smiled an
   old-timer in Wyoming moonlight.
On tiptoe and whispering so no one else could hear, a little girl at
   Brownsville spoke into the ear of the chief executive of the
   great State of Texas: "How does it feel to be Governor?"
Why when the stock crash came did the man in black silk pa-
   jamas let himself headfirst off a fire escape down ten floors to

a stone sidewalk? His sixty million dollars had shrunk to ten
million and he didn't see how he could get along.
"If she was a wicked witch she wouldn't say so, she would be so
wicked she wouldn't know it," said little Anne.
"God will forgive me, it's his line of business,"
said the dying German-Jewish poet in his garret.

The little girl saw her first troop parade and asked,
"What are those?"
"Soldiers."
"What are soldiers?"
"They are for war. They fight and each tries to kill
as many of the other side as he can."
The girl held still and studied.
"Do you know . . . I know something?"
"Yes, what is it you know?"
"Sometime they'll give a war and nobody will come."

One of the early Chicago poets,
One of the slouching underslung Chicago poets,
Having only the savvy God gave him,
Lacking a gat, lacking brass knucks,
Having one lead pencil to spare, wrote:
"I am credulous about the destiny of man,
and I believe more than I can ever prove
of the future of the human race
and the importance of illusions,
the value of great expectations.
I would like to be in the same moment
an earthworm (which I am) and
a rider to the moon (which I am)."

43

Who shall speak for the people?
who has the answers?
where is the sure interpreter?
who knows what to say?
Who can write the music jazz-classical
smokestacks-geraniums hyacinths-biscuits
now whispering easy
now boom doom crashing angular
now tough monotonous tom tom
Who has enough split-seconds and slow sea-tides?

The ships of the sea and the mists of
night and the sheen of old battle-
fields and the moon on the city
rubbish dumps belong to the people.
The crops this year, last and next year,
and the winds and frosts in many
orchards and tomato gardens, are
listed in the people's acquaintance.
Horses and wagons, trucks and tractors,
from the shouting cities to the sleeping prairies, from worn pavements
to mountain mule paths, the people
have strange possessions.
The plow and the hammer, the knife and
the shovel, the planting hoe and the
reaping sickle, everywhere these are

the people's possessions by right of
use.
Their handles are smoothed to the grain
of the wood by the enclosing
thumbs and fingers of familiar
hands,
Maintenance-of-way men in a Tennessee
gang singing, "If I die a railroad
man put a pick and shovel at my
head and my feet and a nine-pound
hammer in my hand,"
Larry, the Kansas section boss, on his
dying bed asking for one last look at
the old hand-car,
His men saying in the coffin on his chest
he should by rights have the spike
maul, the gauge and the old claw-bar.

The early morning in the fields, the
brown thrush warbling and the imi-
tations of the catbird, the neverend-
ing combat with pest and destroyer,
the chores of feeding and watching,
seedtime and harvest,
The clocking of the months toward a
birthing day, the newly dropped
calves and the finished steers loaded
in stock-cars for market, the gamble
on what we'll get tomorrow for
what we put in today—

These are belongings of the people, dusty
with the dust of earth, merciless as
sudden hog cholera, hopeful as a
rainwashed hill of moonlit pines.

25

"You do what you must—this world and then the next—one
world at a time."

The grain gamblers and the price manipulators and the stock-
market players put their own twist on the text: In the sweat
of thy brow shalt thou eat thy bread.

The day's work in the factory, mill, mine—the whistle, the bell,
the alarm clock, the timekeeper and the paycheck, your
number on the assembly line, what the night shift says when
the day shift comes—the blood of years paid out for finished
products proclaimed on billboards yelling at highway travel-
lers in green valleys—

These are daily program items, values of blood and mind in the
everyday rituals of the people.

26

You can drum on immense drums
the monotonous daily motions of the people
taking from earth and air
their morsels of bread and love,
a carryover from yesterday into tomorrow.

You can blow on great brass horns
the awful clamors of war and revolution
when swarming anonymous shadowshapes
obliterate old names Big Names
and cross out what *was*
and offer what *is* on a fresh blank page.

27

In the folded and quiet yesterdays
Put down in the book of the past
Is a scrawl of scrawny thumbs
And a smudge of clutching fingers
And the breath of hanged men,
Of thieves and vagabonds,
Of killers saying welcome as an ax fell,
Of traitors cut in four pieces
And their bowels thrust over their faces
According to the ancient Anglo-Saxon
Formula for the crime of treason,
Of persons covered with human filth
In due exaction of a penalty,
Of ears clipped, noses slit, fingers chopped
For the identification of vagrants,
Of loiterers and wanderers seared
"with a hot iron in the breast the mark V,"
Of violence as a motive lying deep
As the weather changes of the sea,
Of gang wars, tong wars, civil tumults,
Industrial strife, international mass murders,
Of agitators outlawed to live on thistles,
Of thongs for holding plainspoken men,
Of thought and speech being held a crime,
And a woman burned for saying,
"I listen to my Voices and obey them,"
And a thinker locked into stone and iron

For saying, "The earth moves,"
And the pity of men learning by shocks,
By pain and practice,
By plunges and struggles in a bitter pool.

In the folded and quiet yesterdays
how many times has it happened?
The leaders of the people estimated as to price
And bought with bribes signed and delivered
Or waylaid and shot or meshed by perjurers
Or hunted and sent into hiding
Or taken and paraded in garments of dung,
Fire applied to their footsoles:
"Now will you talk?"
Their mouths basted with rubber hose:
"Now will you talk?"
Thrown into solitary, fed on slops, hung by thumbs,
Till the mention of that uprising is casual, so-so,
As though the next revolt breeds somewhere
In the bowels of that mystic behemoth, the people.
"And when it comes again," say watchers, "we are ready."
How many times
in the folded and quiet yesterdays
has it happened?

"You may burn my flesh and bones
and throw the ashes to the four winds."
smiled one of them,
"Yet my voice shall linger on
and in the years yet to come

the young shall ask what was the idea
for which you gave me death
and what was I saying
that I must die for what I said?"

28

In the days of the cockade and the brass pistol
Fear of the people brought the debtors' jail.
The creditor said, "Pay me or go to prison,"
And men lacking property lacked ballots and citizenship.
Into the Constitution of the United States they wrote a fear
In the form of "checks and balances," "proper restraints"
On the people so whimsical and changeable,
So variable in mood and weather.

Lights of tallow candles fell on lawbooks by night.
The woolspun clothes came from sheep near by.
Men of "solid substance" wore velvet knickerbockers
And shared snuff with one another in greetings.
One of these made a name for himself with saying
You could never tell what was coming next from the people:
"Your people, sir, your people is a great beast,"
Speaking for those afraid of the people,
Afraid of sudden massed action of the people,
The people being irresponsible with torch, gun and rope,
The people being a child with fire and loose hardware,
The people listening to leather-lunged stump orators
Crying the rich get richer, the poor poorer, and why?
The people undependable as prairie rivers in floodtime,
The people uncertain as lights on the face of the sea
Wherefore high and first of all he would write
God, the Constitution, Property Rights, the Army and the Police,
After these the rights of the people.

The meaning was:
The people having nothing to lose take chances.
The people having nothing to take care of are careless.
The people lacking property are slack about property.
Having no taxes to pay how can they consider taxes?
"And the poor have they not themselves to blame for their
    poverty?"

Those who have must take care of those who have not
Even though in the providence of events some of
Those who now have *not* once *had* and what they had *then*
Was taken away from them by those who *now have.*

Naughts are naughts into riffraff.
Nothing plus nothing equals nothing.
Scum is scum and dregs are dregs.
"This flotsam and jetsam."
There is the House of Have and the House of Have-Not.
God named the Haves as caretakers of the Have-Nots.
This shepherding is a divine decree laid on the betters.
"And surely you know when you are among your betters?"

This and a lot else was in the meaning:
"Your people, sir, is a great beast."
The testament came with deliberation
Cold as ice, warm as blood,
Hard as a steel hand steel-gloved,
A steel foot steel-shod
For contact with another testament:
"All men are born free and equal."

The cow content to give milk and calves,
The plug work-horse plowing from dawn till dark,
The mule lashed with a blacksnake when balking—
Fed and sheltered—or maybe not—all depending—
A pet monkey leaping for nuts thrown to it,
A parrot ready to prattle your words
And repeat after you your favorite oaths—
Or a nameless monster to be guarded and tended
Against temper and flashes of retaliation—
These were the background symbols:
  "Your people, sir, is a great beast."

29

The people, yes—
Born with bones and heart fused in deep and violent secrets
Mixed from a bowl of sky blue dreams and sea slime facts—
A seething of saints and sinners, toilers, loafers, oxen, apes
In a womb of superstition, faith, genius, crime, sacrifice—
The one and only source of armies, navies, work-gangs,
The living flowing breath of the history of nations,
Of the little Family of Man hugging the little ball of Earth,
And a long hall of mirrors, straight, convex and concave,
Moving and endless with scrolls of the living,
Shimmering with phantoms flung from the past,
Shot over with lights of babies to come, not yet here.

The honorable orators, the gazettes of thunder,
The tycoons, big shots and dictators,
Flicker in the mirrors a few moments
And fade through the glass of death
For discussion in an autocracy of worms
While the rootholds of the earth nourish the majestic people
And the new generations with names never heard of
Plow deep in broken drums and shoot craps for old crowns,
Shouting unimagined shibboleths and slogans,
Tracing their heels in moth-eaten insignia of bawdy leaders—
Piling revolt on revolt across night valleys,
Letting loose insurrections, uprisings, strikes,
Marches, mass-meetings, banners, declared resolves,
Plodding in a somnambulism of fog and rain
Till a given moment exploded by long-prepared events—

Then again the overthrow of an old order
And the trials of another new authority
And death and taxes, crops and droughts,
Chinch bugs, grasshoppers, corn borers, boll weevils,
Top soil farms blown away in a dust and wind,
Inexorable rains carrying off rich loam,
And mortgages, house rent, groceries,
Jobs, pay cuts, layoffs, relief
And passion and poverty and crime
And the paradoxes not yet resolved
Of the shrewd and elusive proverbs,
The have-you-heard yarns,
The listen-to-this anecdote
Made by the people out of the roots of the earth,
Out of dirt, barns, workshops, time-tables,
Out of lumberjack payday jamborees,
Out of joybells and headaches the day after,
Out of births, weddings, accidents,
Out of wars, laws, promises, betrayals,
Out of mists of the lost and anonymous,
Out of plain living, early rising and spare belongings:

30

We'll see what we'll see.

Time is a great teacher.

Today me and tomorrow maybe you.

This old anvil laughs at many broken hammers.

What is bitter to stand against today may be sweet to remember
tomorrow.

Fine words butter no parsnips. Moonlight dries no mittens.

Whether the stone bumps the jug or the jug bumps the stone it is
bad for the jug.

One hand washes the other and both wash the face.

Better leave the child's nose dirty than wring it off.

We all belong to the same big family and have the same smell.

Handling honey, tar or dung some of it sticks to the fingers.

The liar comes to believe his own lies.

He who burns himself must sit on the blisters.

God alone understands fools.

The dumb mother understands the dumb child.

To work hard, to live hard, to die hard, and then to go to hell
after all would be too damned hard.

You can fool all the people part of the time and part of the
people all the time but you can't fool all of the people all of
the time.

It takes all kinds of people to make a world.

What is bred in the bone will tell.

Between the inbreds and the cross-breeds the argument goes on.

You can breed them up as easy as you can breed
them down.

"I don't know who my ancestors were," said a
　　mongrel, "but we've been descending for a
　　long time."
"My ancestors," said the Cherokee-blooded Okla-
　　homan, "didn't come over in the *Mayflower*
　　but we was there to meet the boat."
"Why," said the Denver Irish policeman as he
　　arrested a Pawnee Indian I.W.W. soapboxer,
　　"why don't you go back where you came from?"

An expert is only a damned fool a long ways from home.
You're either a thoroughbred, a scrub, or an in-between.
Speed is born with the foal—sometimes.
Always some dark horse never heard of before is coming under
　　the wire a winner.
A thoroughbred always wins against a scrub, though you never
　　know for sure: even thoroughbreds have their off days: new
　　blood tells: the wornout thoroughbreds lose to the fast
　　young scrubs.

There is a luck of faces and bloods
Comes to a child and touches it.
It comes like a bird never seen.
It goes like a bird never handled.
There are little mothers hear the bird,
Feel the flitting of wings never seen,
And the touch of the givers of luck,
The bringers of faces and bloods.

3 1

"Your low birth puts you beneath me,"
said Harmodius, Iphicrates replying,
"The difference between us is this.
My family begins with me.
Yours ends with you."

"A long, tall man won't always make a good fireman," said the
Santa Fe engineer to a couple of other rails deadheading
back. "Out of a dozen wants to be firemen you can pick 'em.
Take one of these weakly fellers he'll do his best but he's
all gone time you get nine miles. Take a short, stout feller,
low down so he can get at his coal, and he'll beat one of
those tall fellers has to stoop. But if a tall feller's got long
arms he can do wonders. I knowed one engineer used to say
he had a fireman he never saw him throw a shovel of coal
on the fire—his arms was so long he just reached and laid the
coal on!"

He can turn around on a dime.
He has an automobile thirst and a wheelbarrow income.
I don't know where I'm going but I'm on my way.
I'll knock you so high in the air you'll starve coming down.
A bonanza is a hole in the ground owned by a champion liar.
All you get from him you can put in your eye.
He tried to get a bird in the hand and two in the bush but what
he got was a horse of another color.
If the government tried to pay me for what I don't know there
wouldn't be enough money in all the mints to pay me.

59

You can't tell him anything because he thinks he knows more
now than he gets paid for.
It's a slow burg—I spent a couple of weeks there one day.
He bit off more than he could chew.
Don't take a mouthful bigger than your mouth.
Let's take it apart to see how it ticks.
If we had a little ham we could have some ham and eggs if we
had some eggs.
He always takes off his hat when he mentions his own name.
What's the matter with him? The big I, always the big I.
"Why didn't you zigzag your car and miss him?" "He was zig-
zagging himself and outguessed me."
"Are you guilty or not guilty?" "What else have you?"
"Are you guilty or not guilty?" "I stands mute."

32

What the people learn out of lifting and hauling and waiting and
  losing and laughing
Goes into a scroll, an almanac, a record folding and unfolding,
  and the music goes down and around:
The story goes on and on, happens, forgets to happen, goes out
  and meets itself coming in, puts on disguises and drops them.
"Yes yes, go on, go on, I'm listening." You hear that in one door-
  way.
And in the next, "Aw shut up, close your trap, button your
  tongue, you talk too much."
     The people, yes, the people,
To the museum, the aquarium, the planetarium, the zoo, they go
  by thousands, coming away to talk about mummies, camels,
  fish and stars,
The police and constables holding every one of them either a
  lawbreaker or lawabiding.
The fingerprint expert swears no two of them ever has finger
  lines and circlings the same.
The handwriting expert swears no one of them ever writes his
  name twice the same way.
To the grocer and the banker they are customers, depositors,
  investors.
The politician counts them as voters, the newspaper editor as
  readers, the gambler as suckers.
The priest holds each one an immortal soul in the care of
  Almighty God.

bright accidents from the chromosome
spill   from the color bowl of the
chromosomes   some go under in early
bubbles   some learn from desert blossoms   how to lay up and use thin
hoardings of night mist

In an old French town
the mayor ordered the people
to hang lanterns in front of their houses
which the people did
but the lanterns gave no light
so the mayor ordered they must
put candles in the lanterns
which the people did
but the candles in the lanterns gave no light
whereupon the mayor ordered
they must light the candles in the lanterns
which the people did
and thereupon there was light.

The cauliflower is a cabbage with a college education.
All she needs for housekeeping is a can opener.
    They'll fly high if you give them wings.
Put all your eggs in one basket and watch that basket.
Everybody talks about the weather and nobody does anything
    about it.
The auk flies backward so as to see where it's been.
    Handle with care women and glass.
    Women and linen look best by candlelight.

One hair of a woman draws more than a team of horses.

Blessed are they who expect nothing for they shall not be disappointed.

You can send a boy to college but you can't make him think.

The time to sell is when you have a customer.

Sell the buffalo hide after you have killed the buffalo.

The more you fill a barrel the more it weighs unless you fill it with holes.

A pound of iron or a pound of feathers weighs the same.

Those in fear they may cast pearls before swine are often lacking in pearls.

May you live to eat the hen that scratches over your grave.

He seems to think he's the frog's tonsils but he looks to me like a plugged nickel.

If you don't like the coat bring back the vest and I'll give you a pair of pants.

The coat and the pants do the work but the vest gets the gravy.

"You are singing an invitation to summer," said the teacher, "you are not defying it to come."

"Sargeant, if a private calls you
a dam fool, what of it?"
"I'd throw him in the guard house."
"And if he just thinks you're a dam
fool and don't say it, then what?"
"Nothing."
"Well, let it go at that."

The white man drew a small circle in the sand
and told the red man, "This is what the Indian

knows," and drawing a big circle around the
small one, "This is what the white man knows."
The Indian took the stick and swept an immense
ring around both circles: "This is where the
white man and the red man know nothing."

On the long dirt road from Nagadoches to Austin
the pioneer driving a yoke of oxen and a cart
met a heavy man in a buggy driving a team
of glossy black horses.
    "I am Sam Houston, Governor of the State of Texas,
       and I order you to turn out of the road for me."
    "I am an American citizen and a taxpayer of Texas
       and I have as much right to the road as you."
    "That is an intelligent answer and I salute you
       and I will turn out of the road for you."

What did they mean with that Iowa epitaph:
    "She averaged well for this vicinity"?
And why should the old Des Moines editor
    say they could write on his gravestone:
    "He et what was sot before him"?

"I never borrowed your umbrella," said a
    borrower, "and if I did I brought it back."
He was quiet as a wooden-legged man on a tin
    roof and busy as a one-armed paper-hanger
    with the hives.
When a couple of fried eggs were offered the
    new hired man he said, "I don't dirty my
    plate for less than six."

Why did the top sergeant tell the rookie, "Put
	on your hat, here comes a woodpecker"?
"Whiskey," taunted the Irish orator, "whiskey
	it is that makes you shoot at the landlords
	—and miss 'em!"
"Unless you learn," said the father to the son,
	"how to tell a horse chestnut from a chest-
	nut horse you may have to live on soup made
	from the shadow of a starved pigeon."
Said Oscar neither laughing nor crying: "We fed
	the rats to the cats and the cats to the rats
	and was just getting into the big money when
	the whole thing went blooey on account of the
	overproduction of rats and cats."

	Where you been so long?
	What good wind blew you in?
Snow again, kid, I didn't get your drift.
Everything now is either swell or lousy.
"It won't be long now," was answered,
	"The worst is yet to come."
Of the dead merchant prince whose holdings
	were colossal the ditch-digger queried,
	"How much did he leave? All of it."

	"What do you want to be?"
	T. R. asked.
	Bruere answered, "Just an
	earthworm turning over a
	little of the soil near me."

"Great men never feel great,"
say the Chinese.
"Small men never feel small."

33

Remember the chameleon. He was a well-behaved chameleon and nothing could be brought against his record. As a chameleon he had done the things that should have been done and left undone the things that should have been left undone. He was a first-class unimpeachable chameleon and nobody had anything on him. But he came to a Scotch plaid and tried to cross it. In order to cross he had to imitate six different yarn colors, first one and then another and back to the first or second. He was a brave chameleon and died at the crossroads true to his chameleon instincts.

What kind of a liar are you?

People lie because they don't remember clear what they saw.

People lie because they can't help making a story better than it was the way it happened.

People tell "white lies" so as to be decent to others.

People lie in a pinch, hating to do it, but lying on because it might be worse.

And people lie just to be liars for a crooked personal gain.

What sort of a liar are you?

Which of these liars are you?

34

If you can imagine love letters written back and forth between
Mary Magdalene and Judas Iscariot, if you can see Napoleon
dying and saying he was only a sawdust emperor and an imi-
tation of the real thing, if you can see judges step down from
the bench and take death sentences from murderers sitting
in black robes, if you can see big thieves protected by law
acknowledging to petty thieves handcuffed and convicted
that they are both enemies of society, if you can vision an
opposite for every reality, then you can shake hands with
yourself and murmur, "Pardon my glove, what were we saying when interrupted?"

35

The sea moves always, the wind moves always.
They want and want and there is no end to their wanting.
What they sing is the song of the people.
Man will never arrive, man will be always on the way.
It is written he shall rest but never for long.
The sea and the wind tell him he shall be lonely, meet love, be
     shaken with struggle, and go on wanting.

"When I was born in the Chicago Lying-in Hospital," said the
     pioneer's grandson, "there was a surgeon with multiple in-
     struments, two nurses in starched uniforms with silk, gauze,
     antiseptics, and the obliterating cone of the grateful anes-
     thesia. When my grandfather was born in the naked corn-
     lands of Nebraska there was only a granny woman with a
     few clean rags and a pail of warm water."

You can go now yes go now. Go east or west, go north or south,
     you can go now. Or you can go up or go down now. And
     after these there is no place to go. If you say no to all of
     them then you stay here. You don't go. You are fixed and
     put. And from here if you choose you send up rockets, you
     let down buckets. Here then for you is the center of things.

36

"I am zero, naught, one cipher,"
meditated the symbol preceding the numbers.
"Think of nothing. I am the sign of it.
I am bitter weather, zero.
In heavy fog the sky ceiling is zero.
Think of nowhere to go. I am it.
Those doomed to nothing for today
and the same nothing for tomorrow,
those without hits, runs, errors,
I am their sign and epitaph,
the goose egg : 0 :
even the least of these—that is me."

When they told those who had no money
"Save your money"
Those who had no money flashed back
"Would you ask those with nothing to eat
  to eat less?"

"The stairway of time ever echoes
with the wooden shoe going up
the polished boot coming down."

　　Ghost and rich man:
"What do you see out of the window?"
"The people."
"And what do you see in the mirror?"
"Myself."
"Yet the glass in the mirror is the
  same only it is silvered."

"If I am a queen and you are a queen,
  who fetches the water?" inquire the
Hindus, the Turks asking: "If you are
a gentleman and I am a gentleman, who
will milk the cow?" and the Irish:
"If you're a lady and I'm a lady,
  who'll put the sow out of the house?"

"The man put green spectacles on his cow and fed her sawdust.
  Maybe she would believe it was grass.
  But she didn't. She died on him."

When the horses gagged at going farther up the steep hill, the
    driver shouted:
        "First class passengers, keep your seats.
        Second class passengers, get out and walk.
        Third class passengers, get out and shove."

Said the scorpion of hate: "The poor hate the rich. The rich hate
    the poor. The south hates the north. The west hates the east.
    The workers hate their bosses. The bosses hate their workers.
    The country hates the towns. The towns hate the country.
    We are a house divided against itself. We are millions of
    hands raised against each other. We are united in but one
    aim—getting the dollar. And when we get the dollar we em-
    ploy it to get more dollars."

37

"So you want to divide all the money there is
  and give every man his share?"
"That's it. Put it all in one big pile and split
  it even for everybody."
"And the land, the gold, silver, oil, copper, you want
  that divided up?"
"Sure—an even whack for all of us."
"Do you mean that to go for horses and cows?"
"Sure—why not?"
"And how about pigs?"
"Oh to hell with you—you know I got a couple of
  pigs."

    In the night and the mist these voices:
What is mine is mine and I am going to keep it.
What is yours is yours and you are welcome to keep it.
You will have to fight me to take from me what is mine.
Part of what is mine is yours and you are welcome to it.
What is yours is mine and I am going to take it from you.
      In the night and the mist
      the voices meet
      as the clash of steel on steel
Over the rights of possession and control and the points:
      what is mine? what is yours?
      and who says so?

  The poor were divided into
  the deserving and the undeserving
  and a pioneer San Franciscan lacked words:

"It's hard enough to be poor
  but to be poor and undeserving . . ."
He saw the slumborn illborn wearyborn
from fathers and mothers the same
out of rooms dank with rot
and scabs, rags, festerings, tubercles, chancres,
the very doorways quavering,
  "What's the use?"

"I came to a country,"
 said a wind-bitten vagabond,
"where I saw shoemakers barefoot
 saying they had made too many shoes.
 I met carpenters living outdoors
 saying they had built too many houses.
 Clothing workers I talked with,
 bushelmen and armhole-basters,
 said their coats were on a ragged edge
 because they had made too many coats.
 And I talked with farmers, yeomanry,
 the backbone of the country,
 so they were told,
 saying they were in debt and near starvation
 because they had gone ahead like always
 and raised too much wheat and corn
 too many hogs, sheep, cattle.
 When I said, 'You live in a strange country,'
 they answered slow, like men
 who wouldn't waste anything, not even language:
 'You ain't far wrong there, young feller.
 We're going to do something, we don't know what.' "

The drowning man in the river
answered the man on the bridge:
"I don't want to die,
    I'll lose my job in the molding room of
    the Malleable Iron and Castings Works."
And the living man on the bridge
hotfooted to the molding room foreman
of the Malleable Iron and Castings Works
and got a short answer:
"You're ten minutes late. The man who
    pushed that fellow off the bridge
    is already on the job."

"What do you want?" a passing stranger asked
a County Kerry farmer.
"What is it I'm wantin'? Me byes and girruls
is gone. The rain has rotted the prathies.
The landlord has taken me pig for the rint.
All I'm wantin' is the Judgment Day."

"The poor of the earth hide themselves together," wrote Job
    meaning in those days too they had a shantytown.
"As wild asses in the wilderness they must go forth, to seek food
    as their task," wrote Job meaning then too they carried the
    banner and hoped to connect with board and clothes some-
    how.
"In a field not theirs they harvest," wrote Job as though in Judea
    then the frontier was gone, as now in America instead of free
    homesteads the signs say: No Trespassing.
"The weaklings groan and the souls of the wounded cry for
    help," wrote Job taking special notice of those "forced to

garner the vineyard of the wicked one," mentioning footless wanderers of Bible times as though the devices of men then too had an edge against the propertyless.

In the Sunflower State 1928 Anno Domini
a Jayhawker sunburnt and gaunt
drove to a loading platform
and took what he got for his hogs
and spoke before two other hog raisers:
        "Everything's lopsided.
"I raise hogs and the railroads and the banks take them away
      from me and I get hit in the hind end.
"The more hogs I raise the worse my mortgages look.
"I try to sleep and I hear those mortgages gnawing in the night
      like rats in a corn crib.
"I want to shoot somebody but I don't know who.
"We'll do something. You wait and see.
"We don't have to stand for this skin game if we're free Ameri-
      cans."

        "Get off this estate."
        "What for?"
        "Because it's mine."
        "Where did you get it?"
        "From my father."
        "Where did he get it?"
        "From his father."
        "And where did he get it?"
        "He fought for it."
        "Well, I'll fight you for it."

38

Have you seen men handed refusals
    till they began to laugh
    at the notion of ever landing a job again—
Muttering with the laugh,
    "It's driving me nuts and the family too,"
Mumbling of hoodoos and jinx,
    fear of defeat creeping in their vitals—
Have you never seen this?
    or do you kid yourself
    with the fond soothing syrup of four words
    "Some folks won't work"??
Of course some folks won't work—
    they are sick or wornout or lazy
    or misled with the big idea
the idle poor should imitate the idle rich.

Have you seen women and kids
    step out and hustle for the family
    some in night life on the streets
    some fighting other women and kids
    for the leavings of fruit and vegetable markets
    or searching alleys and garbage dumps for scraps?

Have you seen them with savings gone
    furniture and keepsakes pawned
    and the pawntickets blown away in cold winds?
    by one letdown and another ending
    in what you might call slums—

To be named perhaps in case reports
    and tabulated and classified
    among those who have crossed over
    from the employables into the *un*employables?

What is the saga of the employables?
    what are the breaks they get?
What are the dramas of personal fate
    spilled over from industrial transitions?
    what punishments handed bottom people
    who have wronged no man's house
    or things or person?

    Stocks are property, yes.
    Bonds are property, yes.
Machines, land, buildings, are property, yes.
    A job is property,
    no, nix, nah nah.

The rights of property are guarded
    by ten thousand laws and fortresses.
The right of a man to live by his work—
        what is this right?
        and why does it clamor?
        and who can hush it
        so it will stay hushed?
        and why does it speak
        and though put down speak again
        with strengths out of the earth?

39

There have been thousands of Andy Adams
only Andy was one of the few who had the words.
"Our men were plainsmen and were at home
 as long as they could see the North Star."
They got his drift when he laughed:
"Blankets? Never use them. Sleep on your belly and
	cover it with your back and get up with the
	birds in the morning.
"Saddles? Every good cowman takes his saddle
	wherever he goes though he may not have
	clothes enough to dust a fiddle."
They could ride long hours in rain and sleet dozing
	and taking short sleeps in their saddles, resting
	to linger over their morning coffee.
This breed of men gone to a last roundup?
They will be heard from.
They tell us now any Texas girl is worth marrying.
"No matter what happens, she has seen worse."

	In oak and walnut
Those old New England carpenters hoisted and
	wrought.
Sunup till sundown they hoisted and wrought in
	oak and walnut.
Wood had a meaning and wood spoke to the feel of
	the fingers.
The hammer handles and the handwrought nails
	somehow had blessings.

And they are gone now? their blood is no longer
    alive and speaking?
They no longer come through telling of the hands
    of man having craft?
Let their beds and staircases, chairs and gables now
    lingering testify:
The strong workman whose blood goes into his
    work no more dies than the people die.

> "I'm holding my own,"
>   said more than one pioneer.
> "I didn't have anything
>   when I landed here
>   and I ain't got anything now
>   but I got some hope left.
>   I ain't lost hope yet.
>   I'm a wanter and a hoper."

40

"We live only once."

Of course the people buy great big hump-backed
double-jointed fresh-roasted peanuts at ten
a sack folks ten a sack—

Of course the people go to see the greatest
aggregation of concatenated curiosities and
monstrosities ever assembled beneath one
canvas—

Of course they enjoy the oily slant-eyed spieler
with his slick bazoo selling tickets and gab-
bing One at a time please One at a time,
and inside the tent Tom Thumb and Jumbo,
the hippodrome charioteers, the clowns and
tumblers, the lighted pink moment when a
lithe woman is flung into empty air from
one flying trapeze to another.

"We live only once."

Of course the greatest showman on earth who
excused himself with saying, "The people
love to be humbugged," was himself humbugged and lost the first of his fortunes to
the fate that humbugged him out of it.

> Do this, buy now, go here,
> stand up, come down, watch
> me and you will see I have
> nothing up my sleeve and I
> merely execute a twist of

the wrist and a slight mo-
tion of the hand. Do this,
buy now, go here, plans,
programs, inventions, promises,
games, commands, suggestions,
hints, insinuations, pour
from professional schemers
into the ears of the people.

41

"Why did the children
put beans in their ears
when the one thing we told the children
they must not do
was put beans in their ears?"

"Why did the children
pour molasses on the cat
when the one thing we told the children
they must not do
was pour molasses on the cat?"

42

Why repeat? I heard you the first time.
You can lead a horse to water, if you've
 got the horse.
The rooster and the horse agreed not to
 step on each other's feet.
The caterpillar is a worm in a raccoon
 coat going for a college education.
The cockroach is always wrong when it
 argues with the chicken.
If I hadn't done it Monday somebody
 else would have done it Tuesday.
Money is like manure—good only when
 spread around.
You're such a first-class liar I'll take a
 chance with you.
A short horse is soon curried.
A still pig drinks the swill.
Small potatoes and few in a hill.
A fat man on a bony horse: "I feed my-
 self—others feed the horse."
No peace on earth with the women, no
 life anywhere without them.
Some men dress quick, others take as
 much time as a woman.
"You're a liar." "Surely not if you say
 so."
He tried to walk on both sides of the
 street at once.

He tried to tear the middle of the street
in two.

"When is a man intoxicated?" "When he
tries to kiss the bartender good-night."

"He says he'll kick me the next time we
meet. What'll I do?" "Sit down."

He's as handy as that bird they call the
elephant.

Now that's settled and out of the way
what are you going to do next?

"From here on," said the driver at an
imaginary line near the foothills of
the Ozarks, "the hills don't get any
higher but the hollers get deeper
and deeper."

So slick he was his feet slipped out from
under him.

The ground flew up and hit him in the
face.

Trade it for a dog, drown the dog, and
you'll be rid of both of them.

There'll be many a dry eye at his funeral.

"Which way to the post-office, boy?"
"I don't know." "You don't know
much, do you?" "No, but I ain't
lost."

43

When we say fresh eggs we mean fresh.

Buying or selling strictly fresh eggs we mean
    strictly.

If eggs are guaranteed extra special what more
    could be asked?

A rotten egg can't be spoiled and a shrewd
    buyer knows an asking price from a sell-
    ing price.

Why do they say of some fellows, "He knows
    all about the Constitution and the price
    of eggs"?

Eggs offered as plain and ordinary means as
    eggs they are not bad.

The egg market punster noted of one buyer,
    "He dozen't eggsspect eggs specked."

Eggs spotted or dirty of course are priced
    accordingly.

Broken eggs can never be mended: they go
    in a barrel by themselves.

What sort of an egg are you ??

Just today or yesterday someone was saying
    you are a good egg or a bad egg or not-
    so-bad or hard to classify.

Under a microscope Agassiz studied one egg:
    chaos, flux, constellations, rainbows:
    "It is a universe in miniature."

44

Why should any man try to find the distance to the moon by guessing half way and then multiplying by two?

To never see a fool you lock yourself in your room and smash the looking glass.

The new two dollar a day street-sprinkler driver took his job so serious he went right on driving while the rain poured down.

"What! you saw a man drowning and didn't help him?" "Well, he didn't ask me to."

"Help! help! I'm drowning." "Tuesday is the day I help the drowning and I'll be here Tuesday."

"The peacock has a beautiful tail," said the other birds. "But look at those legs! and what a voice!"

The farther up the street you go the tougher they get and I live in the last house.

There's only two in the country and I'm both of 'em.

I can live without you in the daytime but oh when that evening sun goes down it's nighttime that's killing me.

When the hotel waitress saw the traveling man eat fourteen ears of corn-on-the-cob one summer noon in the horse-and-buggy days, she asked, "Don't you think it would be cheaper for you to board at a livery-stable?"

The fresh young hotel clerk pulled a fast one on the internationally famous scientist who asked if they had an Encyclopaedia Britannica in the house: "No, we haven't, but what is it you'd like to know?"

The degree B.B.D.P.B.B.B. means Big Bass Drum Player Boston Brass Band.

86

The letter of recommendation read, "This man worked for me one week and I am satisfied."

If he had a little more sense he'd be a half-wit.

He opened his mouth and put his foot in it.

"Do you think it will rain?" "Be a long dry spell if it don't."

"Got enough, sonny?" "No, but I've got down to where it don't taste good any more."

Yesterday's hits win no runs today.

Nothing is so dead as yesterday's newspaper.

Do right by any man and don't write any woman.

The best throw of the dice is to throw 'em away.

"Give me something to eat," grinned a hobo. "I'm so thirsty I don't know where I'm going to sleep tonight."

"When he whittles toward him he's in good humor, but let him alone when he cuts the other way," they said of a Union Stockyards pioneer.

"And now," said the justice of the peace, "by the authority of the State of Wisconsin in me vested I do hereby pronounce you man and woman."

"Don't analyze me—please," the stenographer pleaded. "Sometimes when I think about you I'm afraid my heart will strip a gear."

45

They have yarns
Of a skyscraper so tall they had to put hinges
On the two top stories so to let the moon go by,
Of one corn crop in Missouri when the roots
Went so deep and drew off so much water
The Mississippi riverbed that year was dry,
Of pancakes so thin they had only one side,
Of "a fog so thick we shingled the barn and six feet out on the fog,"
Of Pecos Pete straddling a cyclone in Texas and riding it to the west coast where "it rained out under him,"
Of the man who drove a swarm of bees across the Rocky Mountains and the Desert "and didn't lose a bee,"
Of a mountain railroad curve where the engineer in his cab can touch the caboose and spit in the conductor's eye,
Of the boy who climbed a cornstalk growing so fast he would have starved to death if they hadn't shot biscuits up to him,
Of the old man's whiskers: "When the wind was with him his whiskers arrived a day before he did,"
Of the hen laying a square egg and cackling, "Ouch!" and of hens laying eggs with the dates printed on them,
Of the ship captain's shadow: it froze to the deck one cold winter night,
Of mutineers on that same ship put to chipping rust with rubber hammers,
Of the sheep counter who was fast and accurate: "I just count their feet and divide by four,"
Of the man so tall he must climb a ladder to shave himself,

Of the runt so teeny-weeny it takes two men and a boy to see him,

Of mosquitoes: one can kill a dog, two of them a man,

Of a cyclone that sucked cookstoves out of the kitchen, up the chimney flue, and on to the next town,

Of the same cyclone picking up wagon-tracks in Nebraska and dropping them over in the Dakotas,

Of the hook-and-eye snake unlocking itself into forty pieces, each piece two inches long, then in nine seconds flat snapping itself together again,

Of the watch swallowed by the cow—when they butchered her a year later the watch was running and had the correct time,

Of horned snakes, hoop snakes that roll themselves where they want to go, and rattlesnakes carrying bells instead of rattles on their tails,

Of the herd of cattle in California getting lost in a giant redwood tree that had hollowed out,

Of the man who killed a snake by putting its tail in its mouth so it swallowed itself,

Of railroad trains whizzing along so fast they reach the station before the whistle,

Of pigs so thin the farmer had to tie knots in their tails to keep them from crawling through the cracks in their pens,

Of Paul Bunyan's big blue ox, Babe, measuring between the eyes forty-two ax-handles and a plug of Star tobacco exactly,

Of John Henry's hammer and the curve of its swing and his singing of it as "a rainbow round my shoulder."

"Do tell!"
"I want to know!"

"You don't say so!"
"For the land's sake!"
"Gosh all fish-hooks!"
"Tell me some more.
    I don't believe a word you say
    but I love to listen
    to your sweet harmonica
    to your chin-music.
    Your fish stories hang together
    when they're just a pack of lies:
    you ought to have a leather medal:
    you ought to have a statue
    carved of butter: you deserve
    a large bouquet of turnips."

    "Yessir," the traveler drawled,
"Away out there in the petrified forest
everything goes on the same as usual.
The petrified birds sit in their petrified nests
and hatch their petrified young from petrified eggs."

A high pressure salesman jumped off the Brooklyn Bridge and
    was saved by a policeman. But it didn't take him long to sell
    the idea to the policeman. So together they jumped off the
    bridge.

One of the oil men in heaven started a rumor of a gusher down
    in hell. All the other oil men left in a hurry for hell. As he
    gets to thinking about the rumor he had started he says to
    himself there might be something in it after all. So he leaves
    for hell in a hurry.

90

"The number 42 will win this raffle, that's my number." And when he won they asked him whether he guessed the number or had a system. He said he had a system, "I took up the old family album and there on page 7 was my grandfather and grandmother both on page 7. I said to myself this is easy for 7 times 7 is the number that will win and 7 times 7 is 42."

Once a shipwrecked sailor caught hold of a stateroom door and floated for hours till friendly hands from out of the darkness threw him a rope. And he called across the night, "What country is this?" and hearing voices answer, "New Jersey," he took a fresh hold on the floating stateroom door and called back half-wearily, "I guess I'll float a little farther."

An Ohio man bundled up the tin roof of a summer kitchen and sent it to a motor car maker with a complaint of his car not giving service. In three weeks a new car arrived for him and a letter: "We regret delay in shipment but your car was received in a very bad order."

A Dakota cousin of this Ohio man sent six years of tin can accumulations to the same works, asking them to overhaul his car. Two weeks later came a rebuilt car, five old tin cans, and a letter: "We are also forwarding you five parts not necessary in our new model."

Thus fantasies heard at filling stations in the midwest. Another relates to a Missouri mule who took aim with his heels at an automobile rattling by. The car turned a somersault, lit next a fence, ran right along through a cornfield till it came to a gate, moved onto the road and went on its way as though nothing had happened. The mule heehawed with desolation, "What's the use?"

Another tells of a farmer and his family stalled on a railroad crossing, how they jumped out in time to see a limited express knock it into flinders, the farmer calling, "Well, I always did say that car was no shucks in a real pinch."

When the Masonic Temple in Chicago was the tallest building in the United States west of New York, two men who would cheat the eyes out of you if you gave 'em a chance, took an Iowa farmer to the top of the building and asked him, "How is this for high?" They told him that for $25 they would go down in the basement and turn the building around on its turn-table for him while he stood on the roof and saw how this seventh wonder of the world worked. He handed them $25. They went. He waited. They never came back.

This is told in Chicago as a folk tale, the same as the legend of Mrs. O'Leary's cow kicking over the barn lamp that started the Chicago fire, when the Georgia visitor, Robert Toombs, telegraphed an Atlanta crony, "Chicago is on fire, the whole city burning down, God be praised!"

Nor is the prize sleeper Rip Van Winkle and his scolding wife forgotten, nor the headless horseman scooting through Sleepy Hollow

Nor the sunken treasure-ships in coves and harbors, the hideouts of gold and silver sought by Coronado, nor the Flying Dutchman rounding the Cape doomed to nevermore pound his ear nor ever again take a snooze for himself

Nor the sailor's caretaker Mother Carey seeing to it that every
seafaring man in the afterworld has a seabird to bring him
news of ships and women, an albatross for the admiral, a
gull for the deckhand

Nor the sailor with a sweetheart in every port of the world, nor
the ships that set out with flying colors and all the promises
you could ask, the ships never heard of again,

Nor Jim Liverpool, the riverman who could jump across any
river and back without touching land he was that quick on
his feet,

Nor Mike Fink along the Ohio and the Mississippi, half wild
horse and half cock-eyed alligator, the rest of him snags and
snapping turtle. "I can out-run, out-jump, out-shoot, out-
brag, out-drink, and out-fight, rough and tumble, no holts
barred, any man on both sides of the river from Pittsburgh
to New Orleans and back again to St. Louis. My trigger
finger itches and I want to go redhot. War, famine and
bloodshed puts flesh on my bones, and hardship's my daily
bread."

Nor the man so lean he threw no shadow: six rattlesnakes struck
at him at one time and every one missed him.

46

The gang in its working clothes
the picnic bunch in its best bib and tucker
hicks from the sticks and big town hicks
they sing whatever they want to
and it may be The Old Rugged Cross
or The Old Gray Mare or a late hit.
　　They are hit by the hit songs.
It's a hit only when it hits them.
They soon drop it like a hot potato
or they hold on to it for keeps.
And whenever they keep changing a song
with tunes twisted forty ways
and new verses you never heard of—
　　at last then it's a folk song.

"Everybody is cleverer than anybody,"
　　said a smooth old fox
　　who once ran France with his left hand.

Of the woman born deaf, blind and dumb, the vaudeville
audience asked questions:
"Have you ever thought of getting married? Why has
a cow two stomachs? How much is too many? Do you
believe in ghosts? Do you think it is a blessing to
be poor? Do you dream? Do you think business is looking up? Am I going on a trip?"
And the woman enjoyed answering these questions from
people born with sight and hearing:
"I liked it. I liked to feel the warm tide of human
life pulsing round and round me."
Her face lighted when a burst of handclapping and light

laughter swept the audience.

"How do you know when we applaud you?" they asked.
And she answered the vibrations in the boards of the
stage floor under her feet told her of every shading
of applause.

In the farm house passing another crock of apples,
On the street car riding to the roller coasters,
At picnics, clam-bakes, or the factory workbench
They have riddles, good and bad conundrums:

> Which goes through the plank first, the bullet or the hole?
>
> Where does the music go when the fiddle is put in the box?
>
> Where does your lap go when you stand up? The same
> place your fist goes when you open your hand.
>
> What are the two smallest things mentioned in the Bible?
> The widow's mite and the wicked flee.
>
> Who are the shortest people mentioned in the Bible? Bildad
> the Shuhite, Knee-high-miah, and the man who had
> nothing but from whom even that which he had was
> taken away.
>
> What was the last thing Paul Revere said to his horse on the
> famous ride? "Whoa!"
>
> "Did you hear about the empty barrel of flour?" "No."
> "Nothing in it."
>
> What is there more of in the world than anything else?
> Ends.

They have Irish bulls timeworn and mossgrown:
You are to be hanged and I hope it will prove a warning to you.
I took so much medicine I was sick a long time after I got well.
I can never get these boots on till I have worn them for a while.
One of us must kill the other—let it be me. We were boys
together—at least I was.

95

If all the world were blind what a melancholy sight it would be.

This will last forever and afterward be sold for old iron.

They would cut us into mince-meat and throw our bleeding heads on the table to stare us in the face.

On the dim and faroff shore of the future we can see the foot-print of an unseen hand.

We pursue the shadow, the bubble bursts, and leaves in our hands only ashes.

> "Ah there tootsie wootsie," has its day
> till the good old summertime has gone
> with the kit and caboodle of its day
> into the second-hand bins, the rummage sales,
> and another whim emerges in, "Okay toots!"

The people, yes, the customers,
In short-order lunch rooms they read signs:
>   If the ice-box gets on fire ring the towel.
>   Don't tip the waiters—it upsets them.
>   Eat here—why go somewhere else to be cheated?
>   Your face is good but it won't go in the cash register.
"There ain't no strong coffee, there's only weak people," said one
heavy on the java.

The people is a child at school writing howlers,
writing answers half wrong and half right:
>   The government of England is a limited mockery.
>   Gravitation is that which if there were none we would all
>   fly away.
>   There were no Christians among the early Gauls; they were
>   mostly lawyers.

96

47

Who made Paul Bunyan, who gave him birth as a myth, who joked him into life as the Master Lumberjack, who fashioned him forth as an apparition easing the hours of men amid axes and trees, saws and lumber? The people, the bookless people, they made Paul and had him alive long before he got into the books for those who read. He grew up in shanties, around the hot stoves of winter, among socks and mittens drying, in the smell of tobacco smoke and the roar of laughter mocking the outside weather. And some of Paul came overseas in wooden bunks below decks in sailing vessels. And some of Paul is old as the hills, young as the alphabet.

The Pacific Ocean froze over in the winter of the Blue Snow and Paul Bunyan had long teams of oxen hauling regular white snow over from China. This was the winter Paul gave a party to the Seven Axmen. Paul fixed a granite floor sunk two hundred feet deep for them to dance on. Still, it tipped and tilted as the dance went on. And because the Seven Axmen refused to take off their hob-nailed boots, the sparks from the nails of their dancing feet lit up the place so that Paul didn't light the kerosene lamps. No women being on the Big Onion river at that time the Seven Axmen had to dance with each other, the one left over in each set taking Paul as a partner. The commotion of the dancing that night brought on an earthquake and the Big Onion river moved over three counties to the east.

One year when it rained from St. Patrick's Day till the Fourth of July, Paul Bunyan got disgusted because his celebration on the Fourth was spoiled. He dived into Lake Superior and swam to where a solid pillar of water was coming down. He dived under this pillar, swam up into it and climbed with powerful swimming strokes, was gone about an hour, came splashing down, and as the rain stopped, he explained, "I turned the dam thing off." This is told in the Big North Woods and on the Great Lakes, with many particulars.

Two mosquitoes lighted on one of Paul Bunyan's oxen, killed it, ate it, cleaned the bones, and sat on a grub shanty picking their teeth as Paul came along. Paul sent to Australia for two special bumble bees to kill these mosquitoes. But the bees and the mosquitoes intermarried; their children had stingers on both ends. And things kept getting worse till Paul brought a big boatload of sorghum up from Louisiana and while all the bee-mosquitoes were eating at the sweet sorghum he floated them down to the Gulf of Mexico. They got so fat that it was easy to drown them all between New Orleans and Galveston.

Paul logged on the Little Gimlet in Oregon one winter. The cook stove at that camp covered an acre of ground. They fastened the side of a hog on each snowshoe and four men used to skate on the griddle while the cook flipped the pancakes. The eating table was three miles long; elevators carried the cakes to the ends of the table where boys on bicycles rode back and forth on a path down the center of the table dropping the cakes where called for.

Benny, the Little Blue Ox of Paul Bunyan, grew two feet every time Paul looked at him, when a youngster. The barn was gone one morning and they found it on Benny's back; he grew out of it in a night. One night he kept pawing and bellowing for more pancakes, till there were two hundred men at the cook shanty stove trying to keep him fed. About breakfast time Benny broke loose, tore down the cook shanty, ate all the pancakes piled up for the loggers' breakfast. And after that Benny made his mistake; he ate the red hot stove; and that finished him. This is only one of the hot stove stories told in the North Woods.

48

One of the Cherokees in Oklahoma, having a million or so from oil rights, went to a motor car dealer, looked over the different new makes, and in a corner of the salesroom noticed a bran new white hearse, embellished, shining, emblazoned. "This one for me," he said, and he rode away, his chauffeur driving and himself seated inside the glittering white funeral car. They tell this in Oklahoma as a folk tale. It is.

In Honolulu they have cockroach races and bet on the winner.
In Japan they have grasshopper stables, each grasshopper in a little stall by himself.
In Mexico they sit around a table each man having a cube of sugar and the first to have a fly sit on his sugar wins the money.

Didn't he belong to the people, that Gallic eater and drinker whose will was short and read: "I have nothing, I owe much, I leave the remainder to the poor"?

And why shouldn't they say of one windbag in Washington, D. C., "An empty taxicab drew up to the curb and Senator So-and-So stepped out"?

"The hungry hog follows his nose to the warm swill," said an old farmer.
"He could live on the smell of an oil rag," they said of an old sailor on a tramp steamer.
"When the wind favors you can smell a slave-ship seven miles," they said in days now gone.

"Baby, baby, you will get new shoes at the gate of
        heaven," sing the Mexican mothers to the mu-
        chacho.

"How are crops this year?"
"Not so good for a good year
  but not so bad for a bad year."

"Didn't you hear me holler for help?"
"Yes but you're such a liar
  I didn't think you meant it."

What about that railroad engineer
running on the Pennsy
twenty-two years out of Chicago
leaving his mother $12,000
directing in his will
they should burn his body
as a piece of rolling-stock
beyond rehabilitation or repair
and take the ashes to his pet locomotive
and when they had run her
to the Beverly curve at 87th Street
where the open prairie view was special
and his eyes had so often
met a changing sky of red and gold—
there from the old cab of locomotive No. 8152
they could empty his firebox
they could throw his ashes
strew the last cinders and clinkers
of an engineer, an old hogger

thankful he had lived—
Always when he had rounded that curve
his run was over and he could go home—
What did he have?
They obliged him. Why shouldn't they?
They were glad to. "But he *was* peculiar, wasn't he?"

"Haven't you had a little too much?" the White House guard asked the Sioux warrior who shifted a blanket: "A little too much is just enough."

When Chicago has a debate whether there is a hell someone always says, "Down in hell they debate whether there is a Chicago."

"Too bad you have to work in this kind of a soup parlor," the customer sympathized, the waiter refusing the sympathy: "I work here but I don't eat here."

A short order lunch room in Waterloo hangs up a sign for visiting Hawkeyes: "We eat our own hash—think it over."

A college boarding house in Ann Arbor instructs the scissorbill: "God hates a glutton—learn to say No."

The slim little wiry Texas Ranger answering a riot call heard from the town committee that they certainly expected at least a company of troopers, which brought his query, "There's only one riot—isn't there?"

"Are you happy?" the evangelist asked the new half-convert. "Well, parson, I'm not damn happy, just *happy*, that's all."

49

He was a king or a shah, an ahkoond or rajah,
the head man of the country,
and he commanded the learned men of the books
they must put all their books in one,
which they did,
and this one book into a single page,
which they did.
"Suppose next," said the head man, who was
either a king or shah, an ahkoond or rajah,
"Suppose now you give my people
  the history of the world and its peoples
  in three words—come, go to work!"
And the learned men sat long into the night
and confabulated over their ponderings
and brought back three words:
      "Born,
        troubled,
        died."
This was their history of Everyman.
"Give me next for my people," spoke the head man,
"in one word the inside kernel of all you know,
  the knowledge of your ten thousand books
  with a forecast of what will happen next—
  this for my people in one word."
And again they sat into the peep of dawn
and the arguments raged
and the glass prisms of the chandeliers shook
and at last they came to a unanimous verdict

and brought the head man one word:
    "Maybe."

And in that country and in other countries
over mountain ranges where white clouds rested
and beyond the blue sea and its endless tumblers
the people by sunlight, by candlelight, by lanterns
by the new white bulbs spoken to with buttons,
the people had sayings touching the phrase
    "Born, troubled, died,"
carrying farther the one word: "maybe,"
spacing values between serenity and anguish,
from daily humdrum and the kitchen stove
to the inevitable rainbow or evening star,
sayings:

What should I say when it is better to say nothing?
What is said is said and no sponge can wipe it out.
    Ask the young people—they know everything.
    They say—what say they? Let them say.
Have you noticed painted flowers give no smell?
A woman and a melon are not to be known by their outsides.
The handsomest woman can give only what she has.
The miser and the pig are no use till dead.
An old man in love is a flower in winter.
    Bean by bean we fill the sack.
    Step by step one goes far.
No matter how important you are, you may get the measles.
    Wash a dog, comb a dog, still a dog.
    Fresh milk is not to be had from a statue.

Apes may put on finery but they are still apes.
Every man must eat his peck of dirt before he dies.
God knows well who are the best pilgrims.
The ache for glory sends free people into slavery.
He who is made of honey will be eaten to death by flies.
No matter how cheap you make shoes geese will go barefoot.
He drives the wind from his house with his hat.

Wedlock is a padlock.
Take a good look at the mother before
getting tied up with the daughter.
Let a mother be ever so bad she wishes
her daughter to be good.
The man hardly ever marries the woman
he jokes about: she often marries the
man she laughs at.
Keep your eyes open before marriage,
half-shut afterward.

In heaven an angel is nobody in particular.
Even if your stomach be strong, eat as few
cockroaches as possible.
The curse of the Spanish gypsy: May you be
a mail carrier and have sore feet.
Well lathered is half shaved.
A wife is not a guitar you hang on the wall after playing it.
The liar forgets.
A redheaded man in the orchestra is a sure sign
of trouble.
The shabby genteel would better be in rags.

As sure as God made little apples he was busy
    as a cranberry merchant.
It will last about as long as a snowball in hell.
I wouldn't take a million dollars for this baby and
    I wouldn't give ten cents for another.

        Blue eyes say love me or I die.
        Black eyes say love me or I kill you.
        The sun rises and sets in her eyes.
           Wishes won't wash dishes.
        May all your children be acrobats.
           Leave something to wish for.
           Lips however rosy must be fed.
           Some kill with a feather.
           By night all cats are gray.
        Life goes before we know what it is.
           One fool is enough in a house.
        Even God gets tired of too much hallelujah.
        Take it easy and live long as brothers.
           The baby's smile pays the bill.

Yesterday is gone, tomorrow may never come,
    today is here.
The sins of omission are those we should have
    committed and didn't.
May you live to pick flowers off your enemies' graves.
Some of them are so lazy they get up early in the morning
    so as to have more time to lay around and do nothing.
Some of them are dirty as a slut that's too lazy to lick herself.
Let the guts be full for they carry the legs.

The hypocrite talks like a saint and hides his cat claws.

The half-wit was asked how he found the lost horse no others could locate and explained, "I thought to myself where I would go if I was a horse and I went there and he had."

He who has one foot in a brothel has another in a hospital.

When the boy is growing he has a wolf in his belly.

Handsome women generally fall into the hands of men not worth a second look.

When someone hits you with a rock hit him with a piece of cotton.

Love your neighbor as yourself but don't take down your fence.

A fence should be horse-high, pig-tight, bull-strong.

> Except in fairy stories the bashful get less.
>
> A beggar's hand has no bottom.
>
> Polite words open iron gates.
>
> Be polite but not too polite.

50

From what graveyards and sepulchers have they come,
these given the public eye and ear
who chatter idly of their personal success
as though they flowered by themselves alone
saying "I," "I," "I,"
crediting themselves with advances and gains,
"I did this, I did that,"
and hither and thither, "It was me, Me,"
the people, yes, the people, being omitted
or being mentioned as incidental
or failing completely of honorable mention,
as though what each did was by him alone
and there is a realm of personal achievement
wherein he was the boss, the big boy,
and it wasn't luck nor the breaks
nor a convenient public
but it was him, "I," "Me,"
and the idea and the inference is
the pay and the praise should be his—
from what graveyards have they strolled
and do they realize their sepulchral manners
and what are the farther backgrounds?

Desecrate the landscape with your billboards, gentlemen,
Let no green valleys meet the beholder's eye without
Your announcements of gas, oil, beans, soup, whiskey, beer,
Your proclamations of shaving cream, tooth-paste, pills, tonics.
On the rocks and rugged hills, along clear streams and pastures

Set up your billboard brag and swagger, your raucous yells.
Desecrate the landscape, gentlemen, go to it, hit 'em in the eye.
Sell 'em. Make 'em eat it. Sell 'em the name, the idea, the habit.
If a rock stands proud and grand anywhere sling your signs up
    on it.

      The machine yes the machine
      never wastes anybody's time
      never watches the foreman
      never talks back
      never talks what is right or wrong
      never listens to others talking or if
          it does listen it doesn't hear
      never says we've been thinking, or, our
          feeling is like this
the machine yes the machine cuts your production cost
a man is a man and what can you do with him?
but a machine now you take a machine
no kids   no woman   never hungry   never thirsty
all a machine needs is a little regular attention and plenty of
    grease.

            We raise more corn
            to feed more hogs
            to buy more land
            to raise more corn
            to feed more hogs
            to. . . .

Once there was a frontier. Year by year it moved west. At last
    it moved into the Pacific Ocean. Word passed, "The frontier

is gone, there is no frontier any more." From then on no more frontiersmen, from then on only jokers advising, "Go west, young man." This was long after the old-timers started west in covered wagons emblazoned "Ho for California" "Oregon or Death" or "The Eleventh Commandment: Mind Your Own Business." One with a sign reading "Pikes Peak or Bust" came back with another: "Busted by Gosh!" And you can go now yes go now though the old frontiers are gone and the free homesteads are few. Now you can stay where you are and send up rockets, let down buckets. Now with less land you will have less children.

What happened in that buried city they
    found in Africa?
Once it had streets and people and business
    and politics.
Once it saw the weddings of young men and
    women
And the children cried "mama" as the first
    word
And they had news from day to day of food,
    love, work, people.
Now it is covered over with a level of snails,
    hills of snails.
The streets, houses, city hall, department of
    public works,
Houses of money lenders, huts of the poor,
    tabernacles,
Filled up and smoothed over by long proces-
    sions of snails,

Legions of plodding thoughtless misbegotten
    snails.

"Isn't that an iceberg on the horizon, Captain?"
"Yes, Madam."
"What if we get in a collision with it?"
"The iceberg, Madam, will move right along
    as though nothing had happened."

You can't come back to a home unless it was a
    home you went away from.
Between hay and grass neither one nor the other.
Can't you be useful as well as ornamental?
Why don't you go roll a peanut around the corner?
    When did they let you out?
The mules went to ask horns and came back without ears.
When you get hold of a good thing freeze onto it.
    Nothing to do and all day to do it in.
So dumb he spent his last dollar buying a pocketbook to put it in.
    A little more sandpaper and this will be smooth.
Write on one side of the paper and both sides of the subject.
Swear to it on a stack of Bibles and they wouldn't believe you.
    Be not a baker if your head be of butter.
Yesterday? It's a nickel thrown on a Salvation Army drum.
How could I let go when it was all I could do to hold on?
Thousands drink themselves to death before one dies of thirst.
    He didn't have much till he married a hunk of tin.
    There's always a nut on every family tree.
    The mosquitoes organized and drove me out of bed.
We'll fight till hell freezes over and then write on the ice, "Come
    on, you bastards."

The yes-man spent his vacation yelling, "No! no! I tell you No!"

A man having nothing to feed his cow sang to her of the fresh green grass to come: this is the tune the old cow died on.

The man feeding a hatful of doughnuts to a horse explained to the curious, "I want to see how many he'll eat before he asks for a cup of coffee."

"I fired the man," said the new section boss, "not because I had anything agin him but because I had the authority."

"Don't I argue? Don't I sputify?" the backwoods preacher inquired of the complaining committee whose chairman responded, "Yes, you do argue and you do sputify but you don't tell wherein!"

The late riser is asked, "Are you up for all day?"

Shut the door—do you want to heat all outdoors?

He won't go to a wedding unless he's the bride nor a funeral unless he's the corpse.

"May you have the sevenyear itch," was answered, "I hope your wife eats crackers in bed."

He was always a hell of a big fellow in Washington when he was in Rhode Island and a hell of a big fellow in Rhode Island when he was in Washington.

You say you are going to Warsaw (or Boston) because you want me to think you are going to Lemberg (or Buffalo) but I know you are going to Warsaw (or Boston).

He got on a horse and rode off in all directions at once.

Did they let you out or did you let yourself out?

"Why!" said a Republican Governor of Illinois, "Why the Democrats can't run the government! It's all us Republicans can do."

This will last a thousand years and after that to the end of the world.

When a member died the newspaper men of the Whitechapel Club of Chicago gave the toast:

"Hurrah for the next who goes!"

In Vermont a shut-mouthed husband finally broke forth to his wife, "When I think of how much you have meant to me all these years, it is almost more than I can do sometimes to keep from telling you so."

51

The blood of all men of all nations being red
the Communist International named red its banner color.
Pope Innocent IV gave cardinals their first red hats
saying a cardinal's blood belonged to the holy mother church.
The bloodcolor red is a symbol.

A Scotsman keeps the Sabbath and anything else he can lay his hands on, say the English.

A fighting Frenchman runs away from even a she-goat, say the Germans.

A Russian, say the Poles, can be cheated only by a gypsy, a gypsy by a Jew, a Jew by a Greek, and a Greek by the devil.

"If I owned Texas and hell I would rent Texas and move to hell," said a famous general.

"That's right," wrote a Texas editor. "Every man for his own country."

The Peloponnesians pulled these _ong ago, so did the Russians, the Chinese, even the Fijis with rings in their noses. Likewise:

An American is an Anglo-Saxon when an Englishman wants something from him: or:

When a Frenchman has drunk too much he wants to dance, a German to sing, a Spaniard to gamble, an Italian to brag, an Irishman to fight, an American to make a speech: or:

"What is dumber than a dumb Irishman?" "A smart Swede."

These are in all tongues and regions of men. Often they bring laughter and sometimes blood.

The propagandas of hate and war always monkey with the buzz-

saw of race and nationality, breed and kin, seldom saying,
"When in doubt hold your tongue."
In breathing spells of bloody combat between Christian nations
the order goes out: "Don't let the men in the front-line
trenches fraternize!"

> The sea has fish for every man.
> Every blade of grass has its share of dew.
> The longest day must have its end.
> Man's life? A candle in the wind, hoar-frost
> on stone.
> Nothing more certain than death and nothing
> more uncertain than the hour.
> Men live like birds together in a wood; when
> the time comes each takes his flight.
> As wave follows wave, so new men take old
> men's places.

The copperfaces, the red men, handed us tobacco,
the weed for the pipe of friendship,
also the bah-tah-to, the potato, the spud.
Sunflowers came from Peruvians in ponchos.
Early Italians taught us of chestnuts,
walnuts and peaches being Persian mementoes,
Siberians finding for us what rye might do,
Hindus coming through with the cucumber,
Egyptians giving us the onion, the pea,
Arabians handing advice with one gift:
"Some like it, some say it's just spinach."

> To the Chinese we have given
> kerosene, bullets, bibles

and they have given us radishes, soy beans, silk,
poems, paintings, proverbs, porcelain, egg foo yong,
gunpowder, Fourth of July firecrackers, fireworks,
and labor gangs for the first Pacific railways.
       Now we may thank these people
       or reserve our thanks
       and speak of them as outsiders
       and imply the request,
"Would you just as soon get off the earth?"
holding ourselves aloof in pride of distinction
saying to ourselves this costs us nothing
as though hate has no cost
as though hate ever grew anything worth growing.
Yes we may say this trash is beneath our notice
or we may hold them in respect and affection
as fellow creepers on a commodious planet
saying, "Yes you too you too are people."

"When God finished making the world
He had a few stinking scraps of mud left over
and used it to make a yellow dog"
       (and when they hate any race or nation
       they name that race or nation
       in place of the yellow dog).
They say and they say and the juice of prejudice drips from it.
They say and they say and in the strut of fool pride spit in the
       wind.
And the first of the seven rottening sins is this one: pride.
They set up a razzle-dazzle and get caught in their own revolv-
       ing mirrors.

"We are the greatest city, the greatest people. Nothing like us
  ever was."
They set out for empire not knowing men and nations can die of
  empire.
And the earth is strewn with the burst bladders of the puffed-up.

> The best preacher is the heart,
> say the Jews of faith.
> The best teacher is time.
> The best book is the world.
> The best friend is God.

> The three worst waters,
> say the Irish:
> brown rain at the fall of the leaf,
> black rain at the springing of roots,
> the grey rain of May.

Love, a cough, an itch, or a fat paunch cannot be hid.
Love, a cough, smoke, money or poverty, are hard to hide.

Three things you can't nurse: an old woman, a hen, and a sheep.
Three who have their own way: a mule, a pig, and a miser.
Three to stay away from: a snake, a man with an oily tongue,
  and a loose woman.
Three things dear to have: fresh eggs, hickory smoked ham. and
  old women's praise.
Three things always pleasing: a cat's kittens, a goat's kid, and a
  young woman.
The three prettiest dead: a little child, a salmon, a black cock.

Three of the coldest things: a man's knee, a cow's horn, and a dog's nose.

Three who come unbidden: love, jealousy, fear.

Three soon passing away: the beauty of a woman, the rainbow, the echo of the woods.

Three worth wishing: knowledge, grain, and friendship.

Men are made of clay but women are made of men.

An old friend is better than two new ones.

He gets up early who pleases everybody.

Two fools in a house are a couple too many.

"I have forgotten your name" is better than "I don't remember you."

Some can eat nails, others break their teeth on apple-sauce.

"Run home, your house is on fire." "No, that can't be. I locked the house when I left home."

"So now he's dead." "Yes." "What did he die of?" "The want of breath."

There are two good men, say the Chinese, one dead, the other not born yet.

The seller can get along with one eye, the buyer needs a hundred.

The ragged colt may prove a good horse.

The hasty bitch brings forth blind whelps.

He's eaten off many a dish and never washed a dish.

He's the sort that would haul rock with a race-horse.

It would be like him to drown in a spoonful of water.

If he had learned the hatter's trade, men would have been born without heads.

Ugly? Sleep stays away from him till he
    covers his face.
Poor? He can't raise money enough to buy
    lumber for a backhouse.
Big feet? Buying shoes he don't ask for a
    number, he says, "Lemme see the biggest
    you got."

                "Slave, I have bought you."
                "God knows you have."
                "Now you belong to me."
                "God knows I do."
                "And you'll not run away?"
                "God knows."

In the days of the faroff Pharaohs
in the days of Nebuchadnezzar
the king who ate grass
and reconsidered many former decisions—
one of the masters straddling a slave:
      "I think about you often
        and I would be willing
        to do many kind things
        almost anything for you."
          And the man under:
"Almost anything except get off my back."

52

Who was that early sodbuster in Kansas? He leaned at the gate-post and studied the horizon and figured what corn might do next year and tried to calculate why God ever made the grasshopper and why two days of hot winds smother the life out of a stand of wheat and why there was such a spread between what he got for grain and the price quoted in Chicago and New York. Drove up a newcomer in a covered wagon: "What kind of folks live around here?" "Well, stranger, what kind of folks was there in the country you come from?" "Well, they was mostly a lowdown, lying, thieving, gossiping, backbiting lot of people." "Well, I guess, stranger, that's about the kind of folks you'll find around here." And the dusty gray stranger had just about blended into the dusty gray cottonwoods in a clump on the horizon when another newcomer drove up: "What kind of folks live around here?" "Well, stranger, what kind of folks was there in the country you come from?" "Well, they was mostly a decent, hardworking, lawabiding, friendly lot of people." "Well, I guess, stranger, that's about the kind of folks you'll find around here." And the second wagon moved off and blended with the dusty gray cottonwoods on the horizon while the early sodbuster leaned at his gate-post and tried to figure why two days of hot winds smother the life out of a nice stand of wheat.

> In the dry farming country they said:
> "Here you look farther and see less,
>   and there are more creeks and less water,

and more cows and less milk,
and more horses and less grass,
than anywhere else in the world."

White man: "I have no time to do anything."
Indian: "Why you have all the time there
is, haven't you?"

They said to the cows, "When you die we will
wrap you in fine linen sheets."
The cows: "We shall be satisfied if we keep
our hides."

Of one piece of Pennsylvania a Quaker poet wrote:
"God might have made a more beautiful region than Chester
County—but He never did."
An Oklahoma newspaper woman rewrote it: "God might have
made a more beautiful country than Oklahoma—but He
never did."

All flesh is grass. From the sod the grazers derive their food and
pass it on to man. Out of the grasslands man takes his meat
and milk and lives. Wherever is a rich banquet it goes back
to the grass. Howsoever men break bread together or eat
alone it is grass giving them life and they could pray: "Give
us this day our daily grass."
And many, many are the grass families. From oats and corn to
blue grass and timothy hay, from rye and rice to clover and
alfalfa, the grass families are many and humble and hard to
kill unless misused and overdriven. The populations of the

grass are lush and green with care in the sun and rain and recurring seasons. The grass carries benedictions and fables of service, toil and misuse. To whom does the grass belong if not to the people?

53

Come on, superstition, and get my goat.

I got mascots.

The stars of my birthday favor me.

The numbers from one to ten are with me.

I was born under a lucky star and nothing can stop me.

The moon was a waxing moon and not a waning moon when I was born.

Every card in the deck and both of the seven-eleven bones are with me.

So you hear them tell it and they mean if it works it's good and if it don't it costs nothing.

How to win love, how to win games, the spells and conjurations are named for fever, burns, convulsions, snakebite, milksick, balking horses, rheumatism, warts.

"Tie the heart of a bat with a red silk string to your right arm and you will win every game at which you play."

If your right foot itches you will soon start on a journey, if it's your left foot you will go where you are not wanted.

If you sing before breakfast you will cry before night, if you sneeze before breakfast you will see your true love before Saturday night.

Lightning in the north means rain, lightning in the south means dry weather.

Frost three months after the first katydid is heard. Three white frosts and then a rain.

For toothache the faith doctor wrote the words "galla gaffa gassa" on the wall. With a nail he pointed at each letter of the words, asking if the toothache was better. At the letter where the tooth was feeling easier he drove the nail in and the tooth stopped aching. Galla gaffa gassa. Gassa galla gaffa.

> Goofer dust comes from the goofer tree.
> Sprinkle it in the shoes of the woman you love and
>> she can never get away from you.
>>> Galla gaffa gassa.

> Even a lousy cur has his lucky days.
> Sweep dirt out of the door after night and
>> you sweep yourself out of a home.
> Shake the tablecloth out of doors after sunset
>> and you will never marry.
> The first to drive a hearse is the next to die.
> Kill cats, dogs or frogs and you die in rags.
> Point at a shooting star or even speak of it and
>> you lose your next wish.

> Better born lucky than rich.
> Marry in May, repent always.
> May is the month to marry bad wives.

> The son of the white hen brings luck.
> So does a horse with four white feet.

> He planted gravel and up came potatoes.
> When a bitch litters pigs that is luck.
> The lucky fellow gets eggs from his rooster
>> and his hen eggs have two yolks.
> Luck for the few, death for the many.

124

Ladders of luck, let us
climb your yellow rungs.
Ropes of the up-and-up
send us silver sky-hooks.
Black horses, let us saddle
you with silk belly-bands.
Black cats with orange spots
bring us big ships loaded
with wild Spanish women.
Galloping cubes of fate
hand us sevens elevens
hand us the pretty numbers.
Black moonlight, let a little
of that old gold drop down.

    Black roses? Yes
there must be cool black roses.
Out of the deep night came to us all
    the kiss of the black rose.

54

Tylor believed it important; he put it down; he asks us to read it, to look at it and see what happens.

"In the islands of the Indian Archipelago whose tropical forests swarm both with high apes and low savages, the confusion between the two in the minds of the half-civilized inhabitants becomes almost inextricable."

Tylor dwelt on the tales of men with tails, homo caudatus or satyr, how you hear about them if you go hither and yon over the earth.

"To people who at once believe monkeys a kind of savages, and savages a kind of monkeys, men with tails are creatures coming under both definitions."

The longer you look at it the more the confusions shift in the shaded areas denoting who belongs where.

55

On Lang Syne Plantation they had a prayer:
"When we rise in the morning
  to see the sun plowing his furrow across the elements,
we are thankful.
For the rising of the east moon we have seen tonight
and for the setting of the west moon we shall see,
we are thankful.
And O Lord—
When my room is like a public hall,
when my face is like a looking glass,
when my teeth shut against a silence,
mother do me no good then,
father do me no good then,
sister, brother, friend, do me no good then.
Help us to know—
when our hands rest from the plow handle and lie still—
when we are like hills gone down in darkness—
when our nostrils are empty of breath—
then let us know when we trust in Thee—
            Thou art a crutch to the lame,
            a mother to the motherless,
            a father to the fatherless,
            a strong arm to the widow,
            a shade from the heat,
            a bridge over deep water."

The little lake with the long name in Massachusetts is called:
Chaugh Jog a Gog Maugh Chaugh a Gog Chaugh Buna
Guncha Maugh wherein the red men intended: We own to
the middle of the lake on this side, you own to the middle
of the lake on the other side, and both of us own the middle.

Oh angel, oh angel,
I don't want to be buried in the storm.
Who's going to close these dying eyes?
Dig my grave with a golden spade.
Lower me down with a silver chain.
The coffin lid will screw me down.
I don't want to be buried in the storm.
Who's going to close these dying eyes?
Oh angel, oh angel.

56

The sacred legion of the justborn—
how many thousands born this minute?
how many fallen for soon burial?
what are these deaths and replacements?
what is this endless shuttling of shadowlands
where the spent and done go marching into one
and from another arrive those crying Mama Mama?

In the people is the eternal child,
the wandering gypsy, the pioneer homeseeker,
the singer of home sweet home.

The people say and unsay,
put up and tear down
and put together again—
a builder, wrecker, and builder again—
this is the people.

The shrouding of obedience to immediate necessity,
The mask of "What do I care?" to cover "What else can I do?"
One half-real face put on to hide a more real face under,
The waiting of the hope of the inner face while the outer face
Holds to its look and says yes to immediate necessity,
Says yes to whatever is for the immediate moment—
This is the pokerface of the populace never read till long after-
    ward.

The people in several longdrawn chapters seems a monster turtle.
Heavy years go by, heavy hundreds of years, till a shroud and
    mask drop,

Till the faces of events command the new faces of people,
And new chapters begin with new faces.

Protective coloration is only for birds and moths who take on
    the look of the leaves and bark they live in?
Out of long usage the ruled-over acquire devices by the ways
    of animals who blend with the landscape.
They can drop into long deep sleeps, they can hide out and
    hibernate till a time of release develops.

In the long night streets of snakeline lights
when there is bitter crying for leadership
and no leadership steps forth
is it because the masses and the intelligentsia
both are a wornout soil so thin and acrid
they cannot fling up leaders?
When the creative breath blows not over the waters
and elders are filled with hypocritical effluvia,
when the silent workers in pure science
are considered inferior to public utility manipulators
is this the time for the young to begin movements,
to question the ways of hypocritical elders
in the long night streets of snakeline lights?

      aw nuts aw go peddle yer papers
      where did ja cop dat monkeyface
        jeez ja see dat skirt
        did ja glom dat moll
      who was tellin you we wuz brudders
      how come ya get on dis side deh street
      go home and tell yer mudder she wants yuh

chase yer shadder aroun deh corner
yuh come to me wid a lot uh arkymalarky
    a bing in de bean fer you yeah
how come ya get on dis side deh street
go home and get yer umbreller washed
    den get yer face lifted
dis corner is mine—see—dis corner is mine
gwan ja tink ya gonna get dis f'm me fer nuttin
    nobody gets nuttin fer nuttin
    gwan monkeyface peddle yer papers
ya can't kiss yerself in here   dis is all fixed

Those without a leader perish,
says the Sanskrit,
those without a youthful leader perish,
those without a female leader perish,
those without many leaders perish.

The people pause for breath, for wounds and bruises to heal,
For food again after famine, for regaining stamina,
For preparations and migration to greener pastures, to canaan, to
    america, to the argentine, australia, new zealand, alaska,
To farflung commonwealths lacking precedent or tradition.
They guess and toil and rest and try to make out and get along
And some would rather not talk about what they had to go
    through
In the first years of finding out what the soil might do for them,
In the first winter of snow too deep for travel, or
The first summer when the few clouds showing went away with-
    out rain, or

The day the grasshoppers came and tore a black path where the
crops had stood.

The people is a monolith,
a mover, a dirt farmer,
a desperate hoper.
The prize liar comes saying, "I know how, listen to me and I'll
bring you through."
The guesser comes saying, "The way is long and hard and maybe
what I offer will work out."
The people choose and the people's choice more often than not
is one more washout.
Yet the strong man, the priceless one who wants nothing for
himself and has his roots among his people,
Comes often enough for the people to know him and to win
through into gains beyond later losing,
Comes often enough so the people can look back and say, "We
have come far and will go farther yet."
The people is a trunk of patience, a monolith.

"And the king wanted an inscription
good for a thousand years and after
that to the end of the world?"
"Yes, precisely so."
"Something so true and awful that no
matter what happened it would stand?"
"Yes, exactly that."
"Something no matter who spit on it or
laughed at it there it would stand
and nothing would change it?"

132

"Yes, that was what the king ordered
his wise men to write."
"And what did they write?"
"Five words: THIS TOO SHALL PASS AWAY."

57

Lincoln?
He was a mystery in smoke and flags
saying yes to the smoke, yes to the flags,
yes to the paradoxes of democracy,
yes to the hopes of government
of the people by the people for the people,
no to debauchery of the public mind,
no to personal malice nursed and fed,
yes to the Constitution when a help,
no to the Constitution when a hindrance,
yes to man as a struggler amid illusions,
each man fated to answer for himself:
Which of the faiths and illusions of mankind
must I choose for my own sustaining light
to bring me beyond the present wilderness?

Lincoln? was he a poet?
and did he write verses?
"I have not willingly planted a thorn
in any man's bosom."
"I shall do nothing through malice; what
I deal with is too vast for malice."

Death was in the air.
So was birth.
What was dying few could say.
What was being born none could know.

He took the wheel in a lashing roaring
hurricane.

And by what compass did he steer the course
　　of the ship?
"My policy is to have no policy," he said in
　　the early months,
And three years later, "I have been controlled
　　by events."

He could play with the wayward human mind, saying at Charles-
ton, Illinois, September 18, 18 58, it was no answer to an
argument to call a man a liar.
"I assert that you [pointing a finger in the face of a man in the
crowd] are here today, and you undertake to prove me a
liar by showing that you were in Mattoon yesterday.
"I say that you took your hat off your head and you prove me
a liar by putting it on your head."

He saw personal liberty across wide horizons.
"Our progress in degeneracy appears to me to be pretty rapid,"
he wrote Joshua F. Speed, August 24, 1855. "As a nation we
began by declaring that 'all men are created equal, except
negroes.' When the Know-Nothings get control, it will read
'all men are created equal except negroes and foreigners and
Catholics.' When it comes to this, I shall prefer emigrating
to some country where they make no pretense of loving
liberty."

Did he look deep into a crazy pool
and see the strife and wrangling
with a clear eye, writing the military
head of a stormswept area:
"If both factions, or neither, shall abuse

you, you will probably be about right. Be-
ware of being assailed by one and praised
by the other"?

Lincoln? was he a historian?
did he know mass chaos?
did he have an answer for those
who asked him to organize chaos?
"Actual war coming, blood grows hot, and blood is spilled.
Thought is forced from old channels into confusion. De-
ception breeds and thrives. Confidence dies and universal
suspicion reigns.
"Each man feels an impulse to kill his neighbor, lest he be first
killed by him. Revenge and retaliation follow. And all this,
as before said, may be among honest men only; but this is
not all.
"Every foul bird comes abroad and every dirty reptile rises up.
These add crime to confusion.
"Strong measures, deemed indispensable, but harsh at best, such
men make worse by maladministration. Murders for old
grudges, and murders for pelf, proceed under any cloak
that will best cover for the occasion. These causes amply
account for what has happened in Missouri."

Early in '64 the Committee of the New York Workingman's
Democratic Republican Association called on him with assurances and he meditated aloud for them, recalling race
and draft riots:
"The most notable feature of a disturbance in your city last
summer was the hanging of some working people by
other working people. It should never be so.

136

"The strongest bond of human sympathy, outside of the
family relation, should be one uniting all working people, of all nations and tongues and kindreds.
"Let not him who is houseless pull down the house of another, but let him labor diligently and build one for himself, thus by example assuring that his own shall be safe
from violence when built."

Lincoln? did he gather
the feel of the American dream
and see its kindred over the earth?

"As labor is the common burden of our race,
so the effort of some to shift
their share of the burden
onto the shoulders of others
is the great durable curse of the race."

"I hold,
if the Almighty had ever made a set of men
that should do all of the eating
and none of the work,
he would have made them
with mouths only, and no hands;
and if he had ever made another class,
that he had intended should do all the work
and none of the eating,
he would have made them
without mouths and all hands."

"—the same spirit that says, 'You toil and
work and earn bread, and I'll eat it.' No

matter in what shape it comes, whether from the mouth of a king who seeks to bestride the people of his own nation and live by the fruit of their labor, or from one race of men as an apology for enslaving another race, it is the same tyrannical principle."

"As I would not be a *slave*, so I would not be a *master*. This expresses my idea of democracy. Whatever differs from this, to the extent of the difference, is no democracy."

"I never knew a man who wished to be himself a slave. Consider if you know any *good* thing that no man desires for himself."

"The sheep and the wolf
are not agreed upon a definition
of the word liberty."

"The whole people of this nation
will ever do well
if well done by."

"The plainest print cannot be read
through a gold eagle."

"How does it feel to be President?" an Illinois friend asked.

"Well, I'm like the man they rode out of
town on a rail. He said if it wasn't for
the honor of it he would just as soon
walk."

Lincoln? he was a dreamer.
He saw ships at sea,
he saw himself living and dead
in dreams that came.

Into a secretary's diary December 23, 1863
went an entry: "The President tonight
had a dream. He was in a party of plain
people, and, as it became known who
he was, they began to comment on his
appearance. One of them said: 'He is a
very common-looking man.' The President replied: 'The Lord prefers common-looking people. That is the reason
he makes so many of them.' "

He spoke one verse for then and now:
"If we could first know where we are,
and whither we are tending,
we could better judge
what to do, and how to do it."

58

The people, yes,
Out of what is their change
from chaos to order
and chaos again?

"Yours till the hangman doth us part,"
Don Magregor ended his letters.

"It annoys me to die,"
said a philosopher.
"I should like to see what follows."

To those who had ordered them to death,
one of them said:
   "We die because the people are asleep
    and you will die because the people will awaken."

Greek met Greek when Phocion and Democritus spoke.
"You will drive the Athenians mad some day and they will kill
   you."
"Yes, me when they go mad, and as sure as they get sane again,
   you."

59

The transient tar-paper shack
comes from the hands of the people.
So does the floodlighted
steel-and-concrete skyscraper.
    The rough-lumber two-room houseboat
    is from the hands of the people.
    So is the turbine-driven steamboat
    with ballroom, orchestra, swimmingpool,
    the fat of the land,
    moving in the mid-atlantic ocean.

Every day the people of the city haul it away,
    take it apart, and put it together again.
Every day around the globe and its atmos-
    pheric fringe the people of the earth live
    the unwritten saga of one day.
Today the fishing boats go out and little men
    shade their eyes and study the treacher-
    ous, rolling, free-handed sea.
Today the steel-and-aluminum streamlined
    passenger train cuts through a blizzard,
    the transcontinental planes are hung up,
    and a liner at sea sends a distress wireless.
Today strikes break out where strikes were
    never heard of before, the lumber trade
    stands in fear of steel-fabricated houses,
    and farming in Somaliland is a hazard.
Every hour thousands of six-decker novels

lived, every minute millions of long and
short stories.

Today homes are lost, farms won, cars traded
in, old furniture lacquered, pigs littered,
an albatross shot, pearls lost in Vienna
found in a fishcan in Omaha.

Today jobs landed and lost, contracts signed
and broken, families scattered and joined,
girls after long waiting saying Yes to men
No to men.

The books of man have begun only a short
stammering memorandum of the toil,
resources and stamina of man,

Of the required errands, the dramatic impulses,
the irresistible songs of this given moment,
this eyeblink now.

Every day the people of the city haul it away,
take it apart, and put it together again.

The how and the why of the people so doing
is the saga not yet written.

Is the story true or a make-believe?

In an ancient clan the elders found one of the
younger, a man of dreaminess, writing a
scroll and record.

Where he had picked up letters and the forbidden art of putting down one word
after another so as to make sense, they
didn't know and he refused to tell.

On sheets to be read long after by other

generations he was doing an eye-witness
   tale of their good and evil doings.
And he swore to them: "I will be the word of
   the people! Mine is the bleeding mouth
   from which the gag is snatched!"
So they took and killed him and set his bloody
   head on a pike for public gaze. Who had
   asked him to be the word of the people?
   When they wanted a history written they
   would elect someone to write it as they
   would have it written.

"You will see me surrender,"
   said one old Viking,
"when hair grows in the palm of my hand."

"What are you fellows scared of? nothing?"
   this too they asked the old Viking who said,
"Yes, one thing we are scared of, we are scared
   the sky might come tumbling down on us."

60

The grass lives, goes to sleep, lives again,
and has no name for it.
The oaks and poplars know seasons while standing
to take what comes.
The grinding of the earth on its gnarled axis
touches many dumb brothers.
Time toils on translations of fire and rain into
air, into thin air.

In the casual drift of routine
in the day by day run of mine
in the play of careless circumstance
the anecdotes emerge
alive with people in words, errands,
motives and silhouettes
taller than the immediate moment:

> "You have fourteen sons in the war?"
> "Yes."
> "And you have more children at home?"
> "Five."
> "And they all came one by one?"
> "No, they was four pair twins, two sets triplets."

"I remember," said the fond Irish mother to the white-
headed boy, "I remember when you was nothing but a
beautiful gleam in your father's eye."

"Breath is made out of air," wrote the schoolboy.
"We breathe with our lungs. If it wasn't for our breath we

would die when we slept. Our breath keeps the life going through the nose when we sleep."

Back and forth strode the campaign orator,
back and forth till an Irishman shouted:
"If you're talkin' stop walkin'!
  If you're walkin' stop talkin'!"

The classical orator from Massachusetts had pronounced the
words "Vox Populi" five times in an Indianapolis speech
when one Hoosier Congressman bet another he didn't
know what Vox Populi meant. The money was put up and
the winner of the bet freely translated Vox Populi to mean
"My God, my God, why hast Thou forsaken me?"

"There on the same track I saw the westbound passenger train
coming fifty miles an hour and the eastbound freight forty
miles an hour."
"And what did you think?"
"I thought what a hell of a way to run a railroad!"

"Is you married?" the elder negro asked his son.
"I ain't sayin' I is and I ain't sayin' I ain't."
"I ain't askin' you is you ain't. Ise askin' you ain't you is."

They were ninety years old and of their seventeen children had
just buried the firstborn son who died seventy-two years
of age.
"I told you," said the old man as he and his hillborn wife sat on
the cabin steps in the evening sunset, "I told you long ago
we would never raise that boy."

145

"I am John Jones."

"Take a chair."

"Yes, and I am the son of John
Throckmorton Jones."

"Is that possible? Take two chairs."

"What's the matter up there?"

"Playing soldier."

"But soldiers don't make that kind of noise."

"We're playing the kind of soldier that
makes that kind of noise."

"No, captain, I never stole nothing to eat out
of that chest. Why, captain, when I
looked in that chest to see if there was
anything to eat in it I met a cockroach
coming out of it with tears in his eyes."

"How do you do, my farmer friend?"

"Howdy."

"Nice looking country you have here."

"Fer them that likes it."

"Live here all your life?"

"Not yit."

61

The nickels click off fares in the slot machines of the subway,
   the elevated.

"Fare, please," say the bus conductors to millions every day of
   the week.

Riders they are, riders to work, to home, to fun, to grief, each
   nickel and dime audited and accounted for as current income payable for taxes, overhead, upkeep, rehabilitation, surplus, dividends, flimflam.

To the whang and purr of steel and motors, streets and stations,
   the fares, the riders, with nickels and dimes, go and return,
   return and go.

One in a thousand says, "Whither goest thou?" but mostly
   "Where you going?"

Mostly they are in accord with the Minnesota Swede:

"Maybe I don't know so much but what I do know I know to
   beat hell."

Like tools tested for grinding and cutting and durability, they
   have gathered them clews of wisdom and they talk things
   over in the bus, the elevated, the subway:

   "The penitentiary is to learn to behave better, to think things
      over, it is lonesome."

   "A comedian acts funny and gets paid to make people laugh
      if he can."

   "Shakespeare is the greatest writer of them all, a dead Eng-
      lishman and you have to read him in high school or you
      don't pass."

   "The police pass examinations and then get a club and a star

to show who they are. They keep order and arrest you
unless you got a pull."

"Handkerchief is to carry in the pocket and blow your nose
with and tie nickels in the corner of for carfare and
church."

"Economy is when you save without being stingy."

"Banks keep money when you have some left over. They
let nobody else get it. And they let you take money out
if you pay for it and do what is regular."

"The Constitution tells how the government runs. It is a
paper in Washington for the lawyers."

"War is when two nations go to it killing as many as you
can for the government."

"The army is men in uniforms, they go away and fight till
they come back or you hear from them."

"The president is the same as a king four years signing bills
in the White House and meeting people. He can do
whatever he wants to unless he is stopped."

"Oath is what you swear to in court that you will tell everything God help you and hold nothing back no matter
what."

"Poverty is when you work hard, live cheap and can't pay
up, you figure and you can't tell where you're coming
out at."

"Liberty is when you are free to do what you want to do
and the police never arrest you if they know who you
are and you got the right ticket."

"The past is long ago and you can't touch it. Tomorrow
today will be yesterday and belong in the past, like that,
see?"

The ingenuity of the human mind and what passes the time of day for the millions who keep their serenity amid the relentless processes of wrestling their provender from the clutch of tongs organized against them—this is always interesting and sometimes marvelous.

Daily is death and despair stood off by those who in hard trials know how and when to laugh.

The fox counts hens in his dreams. The eagle has an empire in the air. Man under his hat has several possessions of comedy.

The name of a stub line under the Lone Star banner is The Houston Eastern and Western Texas railroad.

On the passenger and freight cars is the monogram, the initials H. E. W. T.

And nearly everybody in the territory traversed and the adjacent right of way calls it "Hell Either Way you Take It."

The Never Did and Couldn't railway is the N.D. & C, Newburgh, Duchess and Connecticut.

The Delay Linger and Wait is the D. L. & W., the Delaware, Lackawanna and Western.

Come Boys and Quit Railroading ran the slogan of the 1888 engineers' strike on the C. B. & Q. RR., the Chicago Burlington & Quincy Rail Road.

The floors of the new horse stables were translucent tile, the drinking fountains of marble, the mangers of mahogany, the feed-boxes furbished with silver trimmings and inlays.

"Well, gentlemen," said the proprietor to his inspecting friends, "is there anything you can think of that is lacking?"

"I can think of nothing," said an irreverent one, "unless you want to put in a sofa for each horse."

62

Without the daily chores of the people
the milk trucks would have no milk
the markets neither meat nor potatoes
the railroad and bus time tables
would be on the fritz
and the shippers saying, "Phooey!"
And daily the chores are done
with heavy toil here, light laughter there,
the chores of the people, yes.

In a drought year when one dust storm came
        chasing another across a western town
Out of a Santa Fe day coach a passenger stuck
        his head and queried a citizen
"What's the name of this mean measly dirty
        dreary dried-up low-down burg?"
The citizen responding, "That's near enough,
        stranger, let it go at that."

When the railway stockholder reminded the
        brakeman of orders to call stations in a
        clear tenor voice, the brakeman inquired:
        "What kind of a tenor voice do you ex-
        pect for forty dollars a month?"

The meat wholesaler took in hand one of his
        salesmen: "You've got a bright head and
        your ideas run away with you. Don't be
        so bright when you tackle a customer. Be

dumb. Look dumb. They will appreciate
you better that way."

On a Baton Rouge headstone they carved:
His last words were:
"I die as I lived—
a Christian and a Democrat."

An Arkansas huckleberry cavalry commander
got his men into action with:
"Prepare to git on your creeters—git!"

"How many of yez down in the pit?"
"Five."
"The half of yez come up and be quick."

"Men, will yez fight or will yez run?"
"We will."
"Yez will what?"
"We will not."
"I t'ought yez would."

The restaurant cashier glanced at the check
he handed her and told him: "I am very sorry
but we have an arrangement with the banks
that they don't sell soup and we don't take
checks."

Phone girl: "I'm sorry I gave you the wrong number."
Man: "I'm sorry too, I know it was a perfectly good
number you gave me but I just couldn't use it."

"I'd hate to be up there in that," murmured one studying
an airplane in a tailspin, another murmuring, "I'd hate
to be up there and *not* be in that."

> Man going up elevator:
> "We eat, work, sleep, then we die—eh?"
> Elevator boy: "Yeah."

> The people laugh.
From a light easy humming
to the raucous guffaw and the brutal jeer
> the people laugh.
> The decisions of the people
> as to how they shall laugh and when
> and how loud and at whom and how long—
This is not covered in the vaudevillians saying
every audience is ninety per cent squirrels
and ten per cent nuts and the squirrels are
more to be considered than the nuts; almost
an axiom comes from the same vaudevillians:
what in one hour entertains and goes over big
in another hour starts a riot: the old reliable
jokes fail: hokum demands a new formula:
the query runs, "What are they laughing at this
year?"

"We got butter and we got the Kaiser," taunted the Dutch boy
     across the border.
"We got Hitler," argued the German lad from his side of the
     fence between the two countries.

"We got butter, we got the Kaiser," repeated the Dutch boy, "and we're going to get Hitler."

"Have you a criminal lawyer in this burg?"
"We think so but we haven't been able to prove it on him."

"What's become of your two boys that grew up since I saw you last?"
"One is dead and the other is in the real estate business in Wichita."

"Am I the first girl you ever kissed?"
"No, but I want you to know I am a lot more particular than I used to be."

The Kansas City girl out of finishing school: "If you've got the right kind of a face and personality you don't need the education and if you haven't got the face and personality you can never get education enough."

"Yesterday," said the college boy home on vacation, "we autoed to the country club, golfed till dark, bridged a while, and autoed home."
"Yesterday," said the father, "I muled to the cornfield and gee-hawed till sundown, then I suppered till dark, piped till nine, bedsteaded till five, breakfasted and went muling again."

A farmhand seeing the letters "P C" in a
dream asked if it meant "Preach Christ,"
his pastor counseling, "Perhaps it means
Plow Corn."

Even those who have read books on manners are sometimes a pain in the neck.

If there is a bedbug in a hotel when I arrive he looks at the register for my room number.

They invited themselves to the party: "If you are verandah then we are ashcan."

The fourth time they threw the unwelcome guest downstairs he dusted himself off and called, "I know why you throw me out, you don't want me up there."

At the third stop out of St. Louis where he was again kicked from the vestibule platform, the traveler picked himself up and told an inquirer, "It's nothing at all. I'm going to Cincinnati if my pants hold out."

He sat on a hot stove and didn't say a thing except, "Isn't there something burning?"

The joker who threw an egg into the electric fan soon was stood on his tin ear.

One audience may wheeze like a calliope with sore tonsils and another roar like a burning lumber yard.

Some of them, as you look closer, are slow as molasses in January—or quick as greased lightning.

Some are noisy as a cook-stove falling downstairs, and others quiet as an eel swimming in oil.

They have met salesmen and politicians low as a baboon's forehead, low as a snake's belt-buckle.

Sure as a wild goose never laid a tame egg, they understand a crooked tree throws only a crooked shadow.

They have heard of men trying to keep the sea back with a pitchfork.

They have seen cutups funny as a barrel of monkeys turn gloomy
as a graveyard on a wet Sunday.

They have seen one limber as an eelskin finally locked in like a
fly in amber.

"Sometimes paying on the installment plan is for all the world
like picking feathers out of molasses."

"Crooked as the letter Z, so crooked he could hide behind a cork-
screw, so crooked he couldn't fall down a well, so crooked
he can't lie straight in bed."

The poker party ran through Saturday night and Sunday and
they came out with eyes like burnt holes in an army blanket.

Once in a blue moon something happens so they say it is rare as a
snowbird in hell.

There's nothing to be scared of—unless you're afraid of a paper
tiger.

The woman who'll kiss and tell is small as the little end of nothing.

In the daily labor of the people
by and through which life goes on
the people must laugh or go down.

The slippery roads, icy tools, stalled engines, snowdrifts, hot
boxes, cold motors, wet matches, mixed signals, time schedules, washouts,

The punch-clock, the changes from decent foremen to snarling
straw-bosses, the sweltering July sun, the endless pounding
of a blizzard, the sore muscles, the sudden backache and the
holding on for all the backache,

The quick thinking in wrecks and breakdowns, the fingers and
thumbs clipped off by machines, the machines that behave

156

no better no worse no matter what you call them, the coax-
ing of a machine and fooling with it till all of a sudden she
starts and you're not sure why,

A ladder rung breaking and a legbone or armbone with it, layoffs
and no paycheck coming, the red diphtheria card on the
front door, the price for a child's burial casket, hearse and
cemetery lot,

The downrun from butter to oleo to lard to sorghum, the gas
meter on the blink, the phone taken out, the bills and again
bills, for each ten dollars due ten cents to pay with or nothing to pay with only debts and debts,

The human sardines of the rush hour car and bus, the gnawing
fear of defeat till a workman never before licked says now-I'm-
licked, the boy who says to-hell-with-work-you-never-got-
anywhere-working-and-I'm-going-to-be-a-bum-good-by, the
girl who doesn't know which way to go and has a wild look
about it,

The pleasant surprises of changing weather when the saying passes
it's-a-nice-day-isn't-it and they-can't-take-this-away-from-us,
the shine of spring sunlight on a new planted onion patch
after bright rain, the slow learning of what makes a good
workman and the comfort of handling good tools, the joy of
working with the right kind of a crew and a foreman who is
"one of us," a foreman who understands,

The lurking treachery of machinery, good printers cursing "the
innate cussedness of inanimate things," the pouring of molten
ore at the right nick and the timing of the clutch of a crane
or a lifting derrick or the dump of a steam shovel or the toss
of a hawser from boatdeck to dockpost or the slowing to a

stop for a red light or the eye on the clock for the deadline
of a job marked rush,

The grades and lines of workmen, how one takes care and puts
the job through with the least number of motions and another is careless and never sure what he is doing and another
is careful and means well but the gang knows he belongs
somewhere else and another is a slouch for work but they
are glad to have him for his jokes and clowning.

The people laugh, yes, the people laugh.

They have to in order to live and survive under lying politicians,
lying labor skates, lying racketeers of business, lying newspapers, lying ads.

The people laugh even at lies that cost them toil and bloody ex-
actions.

For a long time the people may laugh, until a day when the
laughter changes key and tone and has something it didn't
have.

Then there is a scurrying and a noise of discussion and an asking
of the question what is it the people want.

Then there is the pretense of giving the people what they want,
with jokers, trick clauses, delays and continuances, with lawyers and fixers, playboys and ventriloquists, bigtime promises.

Time goes by and the gains are small for the years go slow, the
people go slow, yet the gains can be counted and the laughter of the people foretokening revolt carries fear to those
who wonder how far it will go and where to block it.

63

In a winter sunset near Springfield, Illinois
In the coming on of a winter gloaming,
A Negro miner with headlamp and dinner bucket,
A black man explained how it happens
In some of the mines only white men are hired,
Only white men can dig out the coal
Yet he would strike if the strike was right
And, "For a just cause I'd live in the fields
        on hard corn."

White man: "You take the crow and I'll take
the turkey or I'll take the turkey and you
take the crow."
Indian: "You don't talk turkey to me once."

In a corn-belt village after a Sunday game
a fan said to a farmhand second baseman:
"You play great ball, boy, a little more time
  for practice and you could make the big
  leagues."
"Sure, I know it, shoveling cow manure, that's
  all that holds me back."

64

No matter how thick or how thin you slice it it's still baloney.

I would if I could and I could if I would but if I couldn't how could I, could you?

I never made a mistake in grammar but once in my life and as soon as I done it I seen it.

He was a good shoveler but I don't know as I would say he was a fancy shoveler.

"You're always talking about liberty, do you want liberty?" "I don't *know* as I do and I don't know *as* I do."

"The train is running easier now." "Yes, we're off the track now."

The chorus goes, "They take him by the hand, and they lead him to the land, and the farmer is the man who feeds them all."

"I hear a burglar in the house." "Wait, if he finds anything worth stealing we'll take it away from him."

"Did you say the sky is the limit?" "Yes, we won't go any higher than the sky."

"That dwarf ain't worth ten cents to see—he's five feet high if he's a foot." "Exactly, my good sir, he's the tallest dwarf in the world."

The sea rolls easy and smooth.
Or the sea roars and goes wild.
The smell of clams and fish comes
        out of the sea.
The sea is nothing to look at
        unless you want to know something

unless you want to know
where you came from.

The more things change the more they are the same.
The worse things are the better they are.
Things will not get better till they've been worse.
When everyone is wrong then everyone is right.
Everybody was wrong and nobody was to blame.

The windjammer drew into harbor after a long cruise
and they gathered around the captain for a good-by
and they understood exactly what he meant
and it seemed like old times to hear him roar:
    "You can all go to hell
      and I'm damned glad to be rid of you."
Why did they cheer him unless he was one of them?

The Mexicans give a toast:
salud pesetas tiempo para gastarse son,
health, money, time, what are they for but spending?

The hoary English folk saying, "He'd skin a
louse and send the hide to market," is sur-
passed in gayety by the antique Persian
proverb, "He snatches away a flea's hat,"
meaning his calculations are very small,
indeed, indeed. He could sit down and
figure out how it might be possible to
sneak up on a flea, snatch off its hat, and
then by a circuitous route reach a market
place where he would deliver the hat in

exchange for what it might bring from
someone who had a pet flea suffering
for the want of a hat or from someone
collecting flea hats who wished to add
this particular specimen.

Who do you think you are
and where do you think you came from?
From toenails to the hair of your head you are
mixed of the earth, of the air,
Of compounds equal to the burning gold and ame-
thyst lights of the Mountains of the Blood of
Christ at Santa Fe.
Listen to the laboratory man tell what you are
made of, man, listen while he takes you apart.
Weighing 150 pounds you hold 3,500 cubic feet of
gas—oxygen, hydrogen, nitrogen.
From the 22 pounds and 10 ounces of carbon in
you is the filling for 9,000 lead pencils.
In your blood are 50 grains of iron and in the rest
of your frame enough iron to make a spike
that would hold your weight.
From your 50 ounces of phosphorus could be made
800,000 matches and elsewhere in your physical
premises are hidden 60 lumps of sugar, 20 tea-
spoons of salt, 38 quarts of water, two ounces
of lime, and scatterings of starch, chloride of
potash, magnesium, sulphur, hydrochloric acid.
You are a walking drug store and also a cosmos and
a phantasmagoria treading a lonesome valley,

one of the people, one of the minions and
myrmidons who would like an answer to the
question, "Who and what are you?"
One of the people seeing sun, fog, zero weather,
   seeing fire, flood, famine, having meditations
         On fish, birds, leaves, seeds,
  •   Skins and shells emptied of living form,
         The beautiful legs of Kentucky thoroughbreds
         And the patience of army mules.

The sea holds colors in its own way:
below 55 fathoms no black,
below 300 fathoms no red, violet, white, gray,
below 600 fathoms no purple, green, orange:
      "yellow and brown occur at all depths."

   What have you above the ears?
   Or are you dead from the neck up?
If you don't look out for yourself nobody else will.
What counts most is what you got under your own hat.
   Your best friend is yourself.
Every man for himself and the devil take the hindmost.
I'm the only one of my friends I can count on.
   I'm not in business for my health.
   I'm a lone wolf; I work by myself.
   I'm for me, myself and company.
Who said you could work this side of the street?

   God loves the thief but he also loves the owner.
   The big thieves hang the little thieves.
      Set a thief to catch a thief.

Office without pay makes thieves.
The carpenters have sinned and the tailors are hanged.
He must have killed a few to get what he's got.
They'll sell you anything, even the blue sky.
Have you seen one man selling the ocean to another?
A farmer between two lawyers is a fish between two cats.

The rich own the land and the poor own the water.
The rich get richer and the poor get children.
The rich have baby napkins, the poor have diapers.
The big houses have small families and the small
    houses big families.
Why did Death take the poor man's cow and the rich
    man's child?

65

The mazuma, the jack, the shekels, the kale,
    The velvet, the you-know-what,
    The what-it-takes, a roll, a wad,
    Bring it home, boy.
    Bring home the bacon.
    Start on a shoestring if you have to.
    Then get your first million.
The second million is always easier than the first.
And if you get more of them round iron men than you
    can use you can always throw them at the birds:
    it's been done.
Now take some men, everything they touch turns into
    money: they know how the land lays: they can
    smell where the dollars grow.
Money withers if you don't know how to nurse it along:
    money flies away if you don't know where to put it.
The first question is, Where do we raise the money,
    where is the cash coming from?
A little horse sense helps: an idea and horse sense
    take you far: if you got a scheme ask yourself,
    Will it work?
And let me put one bug in your ear: inside information
    helps: how many fortunes came from a tip, from
    being on the ground first, from hearing a piece of
    news, from fast riding, early buying, quick selling,
    or plain dumb luck?
Yes, get Lady Luck with you and you're made: some
    fortunes were tumbled into and the tumblers at first

said, Who would have believed it? and later, I knew
just how to do it.
Yes, Lady Luck counts: before you're born pick the
right papa and mama and the news-reel boys will be
on the premises early for a shot of you with your
big toe in your mouth.

> Money is power: so said one.
> Money is a cushion: so said another.
> Money is the root of evil: so said
>   still another.
> Money means freedom: so runs an old
>   saying.

> And money is all of these—and more.
> Money pays for whatever you want—if
>   you have the money.
> Money buys food, clothes, houses, land,
>   guns, jewels, men, women, time to be
>   lazy and listen to music.
> Money buys everything except love,
>   personality, freedom, immortality,
>   silence, peace.

> Therefore men fight for money.
> Therefore men steal, kill, swindle,
>   walk as hypocrites and whited
>   sepulchers.
> Therefore men speak softly carrying
>   plans, poisons, weapons, each in the
>   design: The words of his mouth were

as butter but war was in his heart.
Therefore nations lay strange holds on
each other; bombardments open, tanks
advance, salients are seized, aviators
walk on air; truckloads of amputated
arms and legs are hauled away.

Money is power, freedom, a cushion, the
root of all evil, the sum of bless-
ings.

"Tell us what is money.
For we are ignorant of money, its ways and
meanings,
Each a child in a dark storm where people
cry for money."

Where the carcass is the buzzards gather.
Where the treasure is the heart is also.
Money breeds money.
Money runs the world.
Money talk is bigger than talk talk.
No ear is deaf to the song that gold sings.
Money is welcome even when it stinks.
Money is the sinew of love and of war.
Money breaks men and ruins women.
Money is a great comfort.
Every man has his price.
There are men who can't be bought.
There are women beyond purchase.
When you buy judges someone sells justice.
You can buy anything except day and night.

66

The poobahs rise and hold their poobah sway
till their use is over
and other poobahs hitherto unheard of
step into their shoes and sit at the big tables
and have their say-so
till events order the gong for them:
and the fathers can never arrange for the sons
to be what the fathers were
in the days that used to be: not for long:
    both the people and the poobahs—
    life will not let them be.
A little bird flits to the window sills
    morning by morning:
"Whither goest thou? whither and whither?"

They die at noon and midnight,
they are born in the morning, the afternoon,
and the river goes on
and the foamflecks of the river go on.
    The same great river carries along
    its foamflecks of poobahs and plain people.
    They and their houses go down the river,
    houses built for use or show
    down the crumbling stream they go—
cabins, frame lumber cottages, installment bungalows,
mail order residences picked from a catalogue,
mansions whose windows and gables laughed a rivalry,
    down the same river they all go.

A few stand, a few last longer than others
while time and the rain, water and air and time
    have their way,
morning by morning the little birds on the window sills:
    "Whither goest thou? whither and whither?"

67

Was he preaching or writing poetry or talking through his hat? He was a Chinaman saying, "The fishes though deep in the water may be hooked. The birds though high in the air may be shot. Man's heart only is out of reach. The heavens may be measured. The earth may be surveyed. The heart of man alone is not to be known."

"Sleep softly, eagle forgotten," wrote an Illinois poet at the grave of the only governor of Illinois sure to be named by remote generations.

"You have no ruins in America so I thought I would come and visit you," said an English lord to a paralyzed hobo poet in Camden, New Jersey.

"The fundamental weakness in every empire and every great civilization was the weakness in the character of the upper classes," ventured a Yale professor in a solemn moment.

"When historians of the future tell posterity what the World War was about, they will agree upon a cause that nobody who fought it ever suspected," said the chief of the high command of the Allied Armies.

"Bring me my liar," said a king calling for the historian of the realm.

"History is bunk," said a history-making motor car king.

"Words," added this motor car king, "are a camouflage for what is going on in the mind."

"History is a fable agreed upon," said a shriveled smiling Frenchman.

"Even if you prove it, who cares?" demanded an Illinois state librarian.

"I shall arrange the facts and leave the interpretation to the reader," said the hopeful biographer to the somber historian.

"The moment you begin to arrange you interpret," emitted the somber historian.

"Do you make your newspaper for yourself or the public?" was asked a New York founder who replied, "For the public, of course."

"Why isn't your newspaper more intelligent?" was asked a Chicago publisher who laughed, "We make our newspaper for boobs."

"Secret influence is the greatest evil of our time," testified a Harvard president from a birthmarked anxious face.

"And," added another world-renowned educator, "the crookedest crooks in the United States government have been well educated."

"Nevertheless," quoth an old-fashioned bibulous mayor of Milwaukee, "this dying for principle is all rot."

"Put a dollar on the shelf thirty days and you have a dollar," said one president of the Pennsylvania railroad. "Put a workingman on the shelf thirty days and you have a skeleton."

"The struggle," said a delegate from the coal miners, "is between stockholders who do not labor as against laborers who do not hold stock."

"The cry of 'Let us alone,'" urged a British commoner, "grows less resolute, more touched with frenzy."

"Thou shalt not steal," added another commoner, "assumes thou shalt not be stolen from."

"To cure the depression," said one adviser early in the depression, "you must put the patient on a rich, heavy diet because he is starving for nourishment and at the same time you must starve him because he is suffering and overstuffed with rich food."

"You make rifles," said an eagle-faced old railroad fireman to ten thousand Chicago workingmen at a summer picnic, "you make rifles—and you're always at the wrong end of them."

"The mystery of mysteries," contributed an engineer, "is to watch machinery making machinery."

"Art," offered an artist, "is something you can't put into words and when you do it isn't art."

"When I am not engaged in thought," said the possessor of one great mind, "I am employed in recovering from its effects."

"Millionaires," said one having two hundred millions, "millionaires who laugh are rare."

"War requires three things," urged a short commentator with a long head, "first, money; second, money; and third, money."

"Man," spoke up an anthropologist, "is a two-legged animal without feathers, the only one who cooks his food, uses an alphabet, carries firearms, drinks when he is not thirsty, and practices love with an eye on birth control."

"On the one hand an ignorant and arrogant government, and on the other hand a gang of ignorant and arrogant hoodlums— so often the voters must choose between these two," said a desperate registered voter in Philadelphia as he put a seidel of bock beer under his belt only two blocks from Independence Hall and the celebrated crack in the silent Liberty Bell.

"For what are we fighting?" inquired a Richmond editor in 1863. "An abstraction."

"Peace and amity," said a Georgian in the same year, "is obstructed by only two circumstances, the landing of the Pilgrim Fathers, and Original Sin."

"Sometimes," offered a Concord hermit building a hut for himself, "we class those who are one-and-a-half-witted with the half-witted because we appreciate only a third of their wit."

"Broadway is a street," typed the colyumist, "where people spend money they haven't earned to buy things they don't need to impress people they don't like."

"You ask me what is my theory of the universe," the physicist replied, "when I haven't even a theory of magnetism."

"The great events of the world," submitted a historian, "take place in the brain."

"In the last analysis," propounded a California wheat novelist, "the people are always right—a literature which cannot be vulgarized is not literature at all and will perish."

"The durable culture of any nation," ventured another historian, "rests on the mind and genius of its common folk, the masses of the people."

> In a hot house room where sunlight never came
> hundreds of monster plants winding and twisting
> and by light and volume turned on and off
> you could make them grow fast or slow—
> you could see them trail in snake-vines,
> explode into mammoth elephant ears.
> They crept and reeled in processions

173

Of obedient giant clowns and dwarfs, grotesques,
Symbols of an underworld not yet organized by man,
Tokens of plenty and hunger in the controls of man
And the master of these dumb clumsy growths,
A dwarf and a hunchback, a deep believer
In the spirit of man mastering material environment,
Out of Schenectady a wizard loving mankind in peak and abyss,
Saying science and invention are the enemies of human want
And the world is organized to abolish poverty
Whenever the people of the world so will.

Mild and modest were the delegates meeting in
      Basle in 1912 and resolving:
"Let the governments remember . . . they cannot
      unleash a war without danger to themselves."
Mild and modest were the delegates meeting in
      Geneva in 1934 and resolving:
"Man is still, of all baggage, the most difficult to
      transport, and so long as the occupational and
      geographical mobility of labor and the effi-
      ciency of its distribution among different ave-
      nues and places of employment are not im-
      proved at a rate corresponding to accelerated
      technical change, there is reason to expect the
      persistence of a higher volume of technolog-
      ical unemployment."

"Listen to me,
     brother.
They'll hand yuh anything.
Look for the dirty work.
     Listen.
Never see nothin'.
Never know nothin'.
Never tell nothin'.
Then yuh'll get along.
If they want to frame on yuh,
          they will."

68

"The drama of politics doesn't interest me," said a news rewrite man between beers. "It's only the people running around trying to change one gang of bandits for another gang of bandits."

"I've written thousands of words about nothing," said rewrite number two, "and I can do it again."

"I don't know anything," chimed number three, "and come to think about it what I do know ain't so."

"What was it the doughboy wrote home?" a Sunday feature writer chipped in. "Pershing stood at the tomb of Napoleon and said, 'LaFollette, we are here!' "

"Next," burbled a city editor, "you'll be telling about the cub who wired from the town on fire, 'All is confusion can send nothing.' "

"Either that," he went on, "or the lad whose assignment was to interview God and be sure to get a picture."

"Or," not yet being interrupted, "the utilities chief who brushed by Saint Peter at the gate of heaven saying, 'I can't bother with you, where's God?' "

"I want money," said the editorial writer who knew where he got it, "in order to buy the time to get the things that money will not buy."

"If the utilities," the Sunday feature writer kicked in again, "could meter the moonlight the lovers would have to pay, pay, and pay."

"I love a few individuals," came a droll desk man, "but I've got a grudge in general against the human race."

176

"Me," came another desk man, "I hate a few individuals and outside of that I love the whole damn human family."

"Hell's bitches," a street man cut in, "are poverty, crime, ignorance and idleness. Disease and insanity are final breakdowns ending long periods of anxiety, fear, worry, and unrest."

"He's reading books, the sonofagun," interrupted the city editor. "He's going literary on us. And how are we going to get out a paper without poverty and crime?"

"I found out it takes a smart man to be a crook," said a new lad on the police run. "And then I got to asking why should a smart man want to be a crook? He doesn't have to."

"The way to be a big shot is don't know too much," a desk man offered. "What you don't know won't hurt you."

"Man," said a hitherto silent Sunday feature writer, "is infinitely more important than the property he creates. We cannot separate the individual from the work it produces. Property does not exist outside and above the men who jointly produce it."

"He'll be joining the guild soon if he hasn't already got a card," the editorial writer editorialized. "Bend thy neck, proud Sicambrian. Adore what thou hast burned. Burn what thou hast adored."

"May," a rewrite ended the session, "may the fair goddess, Fortune, fall deep in love with thee and prosperity be thy page."

"If you have nothing to do please don't do it here," said one of the rewrites opening the next day's session with a tall tankard.

"Nevertheless," rejoined a rewrite, "I can tell you I met a discouraged undertaker today saying his business was to bury the dead and it looked to him as though the dead have stopped dying."

"And I," put in a member of the art department, "met an intellectual who says to me why don't you draw the pelican and all I could hand him was why do I want to draw the pelican since it's all there when you look at it and any of the camera boys can do it quicker."

One camera boy saying, "I have found woman to be the same as man, with slight alterations," another burbled, "Thank God for those alterations."

"I don't see," put in the new college lad on the police run, "why any man wants to kill another. If he'll just wait the other man is going to die sometime anyhow."

"It's like men chasing after women," said a rewrite. "If they didn't the women would chase after them."

"We ought to have a series of interviews," offered a desk man, "on whether the man chases the woman or whether it's the woman that chases the man, columns and columns with pictures and snappy captions."

"They put on the wires today," said a unit from the telegraph desk, "an Irish poet saying when he's going to write a poem he has the same feeling a hen has when she's going to lay an egg."

"That's news," believed the city editor. "News is anything we think ought to be printed to gladden our readers' hearts or throw the fear of God into them."

"We describe the revels of the rich," interposed a slightly illuminated assistant Sunday editor, "so the poor may enjoy in imagination the pleasures their purses will not permit them in reality."

178

"Yet I notice," he went on, "my associates have considerable difficulty on various occasions in brightening and rendering readable the dull antics of the wives of the big advertisers."

"And," he continued, "if the big advertiser himself gets into difficulties so notorious that something must be printed we soften the blow to the fullest extent and this is as it should be for advertising is the life blood of a newspaper and who are we that we should bite the hand that feeds us?"

"You're a dirty radical bothered with a streak of the blessed Rotarian," put in a rewrite.

"In Moscow," interpersed one just back from Russia, "an English liberal tells me a bugler every morning steps out in front of the Kremlin and blows a long powerful blast and they ask him what for and he says, 'I am sounding the call for the international revolution of the united workers of the world who have nothing to lose but their chains and a world to gain,' and they ask him what he gets paid for this daily bugle call and he says, 'Not much—but it's a permanent job.'"

"For my part," an editorial writer ended his silence, "I begin each bright morning with praying: Lord, give me this day my daily opinion and forgive me the one I had yesterday."

"And I," rejoined the slightly illuminated one, "never quit dreaming of a time when every man is his own policeman, priest and editorial writer."

"You would wish yourself," the editorial writer had it, "out of your own job and me out of mine."

"Yes," as some of them prepared for the suburban trains, "one of these days science and invention will have rendered each one of us humble servants of the public a superfluous and

179

unnecessary unit of labor and all we'll have to worry about is how to occupy our very valuable minds when there is nothing to do but nothing."

The city editor managed to have the final words.

"I'll take vanilla! horsefeathers!"

69

"A lawyer," hiccuped a disbarred member of the bar, "is a man who gets two other men to take off their clothes and then he runs away with them."

"If the law is against you, talk about the evidence," said a battered barrister. "If the evidence is against you, talk about the law, and, since you ask me, if the law and the evidence are both against you, then pound on the table and yell like hell."

"The law," said the Acme Sucker Rod manufacturer who was an early Christian mayor of Toledo, Ohio, "The law is what the people will back up."

"You haven't climbed very high," said a Wall Street operator who was quoted in the press, "unless you own a judge or two."

> Lawyer: What was the distance between
> the two towns?
> Witness: Two miles as the cry flows.
> Lawyer: You mean as the crow flies.
> Judge: No, he means as the fly crows.

> Between the Whig sheriff and the Democratic judge in Boone County, Missouri, was a breach wide enough to erect gallows.

> A visiting lawyer handed the judge a brief spattered with large goose-quill penmanship.

The judge turned the document crossways
and upside down scrutinizing it.
"Can't that judge of yours read writin'?"
whispered the lawyer to the sheriff.
"No," whispered the sheriff. "He can't
read readin', let alone writin'."

Who was the *twentieth* century lawyer who said of another lawyer, "He has one of the most enlightened minds of the
eighteenth century"? and why did fate later put both of
them on the Supreme Court bench?

The surgeon held his profession the oldest in
the world through the operation whereby
Eve was made of rib from Adam.
The engineer held the world was once chaos
and its reorganization a matchless engineer-
ing feat.
The politician put in, "Who made that chaos?"
And the laugh comes in there, a half a
laugh, and come to think about it, less
than half a laugh.

70

The tumblers of the rapids go white, go green,
go changing over the gray, the brown, the rocks.
The fight of the water, the stones,
the fight makes a foam laughter
before the last look over the long slide
down the spread of a sheen in the straight fall.
    Then the growl, the chutter,
      down under the boom and the muffle,
    the hoo hoi deep,
    the hoo hoi down,
          this is Niagara.

The human race in misery snarls.
The writhing becomes a mob.
The mob is the beginning of something,
Perhaps the mournful beginning
Of a march out of darkness
Into a lesser darkness
And so on until
The domes of smooth shadows
Space themselves in tall triangles
And nations exchange oleanders
Instead of gas, loot and hot cargo.
The mob is a beginning, man lacking concert.
The hanging mob hangs more than its victim.
These seethings are a recoil and a downdrag.
Each debauch costs.
Fevers and rots run a course before growth.

The mob is a beginning, man lacking concert.
What is an army with banners and guns
Other than a mob given form and orders to kill?
And when will the nations exchange oleanders
Instead of gas, loot and hot cargo?

A train of soldiers passes.
The khaki lads cheer, laugh, sing, and the flag goes by.
They are young and the young time is the time to be gay, to sing, laugh, cheer, even out of car windows on the way to mine strike duty.
Some of these boys will be laid out stiff and flags will drape their coffins.
Some of the mine strikers will be laid out stiff and flags drape their coffins.
Faraway owners of the mines will read about it in morning papers alongside breakfast.

71

Who was that antique Chinese crook who put over his revolution and let out a rooster crow: "Burn all the books! history
must begin with us!"

What burned so inside of him that he must burn all the books?
and why do we all want to read those books just because
he hated them so?

Yet we hand him this: He singled out no special lot of books for
burning: he hated books as such and wanted them all up in
smoke.

"Let history begin with us," was his cry and maybe it began and
what were its chapters and what was his name as its be-
ginner?

What is history but a few Big Names plus
People?
What is a Big Name unless the people love it
or hate it
For what it did to them or for them while it
was in the going?
And this Big Name means pretense and plunder,
ashes and dung,
While another is armfuls of roses, enshrined
beyond speech.

You may call spirits from the vasty deep,
Aye, you may—but will they come
When you call them?
You may sell an idea to the people
And sit back satisfied you have them your way

But will they stay sold on the idea?
Will they be easy to hold in line
Unless the idea has a promise of roots
Twisted deep in the heart of man
Being brought into play
As though justice between man and man
May yet breeze across the world with sea-smells
And a very old, a very plain homemade cry,
"Why didn't we think of this before?"

In the intimate circles of the dictator,
At the desk at the end of a long room
     where the imitation of God Almighty
     sits running the works,
In the speech and look of the main star
     and the lesser stars hovering in a
     cluster and an orbit,
They know in the pressure of their personal
     ego that this too shall pass away and be
     lost in the long mass shadow of the ever-
     living people
And down under the taboos and emblems, be-
     hind pomp and ritual, posture and strut,
     if the word justice is only one more word,
     if the talk about justice is merely window-
     dressing, if liberty is pushed too far in the
     name of discipline, if the delicate lines
     between personal freedom and requisite so-
     cial performance are not every moment
     a terrible load of care

There will be a payday and little bells lost in
    the clang and boom of big bells.

    People are what they are
    because they have come out of what was.
    Therefore they should bow down before what was
    and take it and say it's good—or should they?

The advocates and exemplars of pride and gluttony
are forgotten or recalled with loathing.
The mouthpieces of dumb misery are remembered
for the bitter silences they broke with crying:
    "Look, see this!
    if it is alive or only half-alive
    what name does it go by,
    why is it what it is
    and how long shall it be?"

            Who can fight against the future?
            What is the decree of tomorrow?
            Haven't the people gone on and on
                always taking more of their own?
            How can the orders of the day
                be against the people in this time?
            What can stop them from taking
                more and more of their own?

187

72

What is a judge? A judge is a seated torso and head sworn before
God never to sell justice nor play favorites while he umpires
the disputes brought before him.

When you take the cigar out of your face and the fedora off
your head in the presence of the court, you do it because it
is required from those who are supposed to know they have
come into a room where burns the white light of that priceless abstraction named justice.

What is a judge? The perfect judge is austere, impersonal, im-
partial, marking the line of right or wrong by a hairsbreadth.

Before him, bow humbly, bow low, be a pilgrim, light a candle

For he is a rara avis, a rare bird, a white blackbird, a snowwhite
crow.

What is a judge? A featherless human biped having bowels,
glands, bladders, and intricate blood vessels of the brain,

One more frail mortal, one more candle a sudden change of
wind might blow out as any common candle blows out in
a wind change

So that never again does he sit in his black robes of solemn im-
port before a crowded courtroom saying two-years ten-
years twenty-years life for you or "hanged by the neck till
you are dead dead dead."

What is a judge? One may be the owner of himself coming to
his decisions often in a blur of hesitations knowing by what
snarled courses and ropes of reason justice operates, with
reservations, in twilight zones.

What is a judge? Another owns no more than the little finger of himself, others owning him, others having placed him where he is, others telling him what they want and getting it, others referring to him as "our judge" as though he is measured and weighed beforehand the same as a stockyards hog, others holding him to decisions evasive of right or wrong, others writing his decisions for him, the atmosphere hushed and guarded, the atmosphere having a faint stockyards perfume.

What is a judge? Sometimes a mind giving one side the decision and the other side a lot of language and sympathy, sometimes washing his hands and rolling a pair of bones and leaving equity to a pair of galloping ivories.

What is a judge? A man picked for a job by politicians with an eye sometimes on justice for the public, equal rights to all persons entering—or again with an eye on lucrative favors and special accommodations—a man having bowels, glands, bladder, and intricate blood vessels of the brain.

Take that cigar out of your face. Take that hat off your head.

And why? why? Because here we are sworn never to sell justice and here burns the white light of that priceless abstraction named justice.

> What is a judge?
> He is a man.
> Yes, after all, and no matter what,
> and beyond all procedures and investitures,
> a judge is nothing more nor less than a man—
>> one man having his one-man path, his one-
>> man circle and orbit among other men

each of whom is one man.

Therefore should any judge open his mouth
and speak as though his words have an
added light and weight beyond the speech
of one man?

Of what is he the mouthpiece when he speaks?

Of any ideas or passions other than those gathered and met in the mesh of his own personality? Can his words be measured forth
in so special a realm of exact justice instructed by tradition, that they do not re-
late to the living transitory blood of his
vitals and brain, the blood so soon to cool
in evidence of his mortal kinship with all
other men?

73

In the light of the cold glimmer of what everybody knows, why
should the owners of the judges speak of respect for the law
and the sanctity of the Constitution when they know so well
how justice has been taken for a ride and thrown gagged
and beaten into a ditch?

Why is it now a saying of the people, "You can't convict a million dollars"?

Why is the bribe-taker convicted so often and the bribe-giver so
seldom?

Why does a hoary proverb live on its allegation that the nets of
the law gather the petty thieves and let the big ones get
away? what does this mean in the homes of the poor? how
does it connect with crime and the poor?

Why should the propertyless depositors of wrecked banks be
saying, "Wreck a bank from the outside and you get twenty
years, wreck it from the inside and all you have to do is
start another bank"?

What do the people say in their homes, in their churches, in
their gathering places over coffee-and-doughnuts beer-and-
pretzels? and how does the talk run about millionaire rob-
bers, malefactors of great wealth, sitting easy with their loot
while

One-two-three, five-six-seven every day the police seize and the
courts order to jail
this skulker who stole a bottle of milk,
this shadow who ran off with a loaf of bread,
this wanderer who purloined a baby sweater
in a basement salesroom—

And the case is dismissed of the railroad yard plain-clothes detective who repeatedly called "Stop!" to a boy running with a sack of coal and the boy not stopping the dick let him have it. "It was dark and I couldn't see him clear and I aimed at his legs. My intention was to stop him running. I didn't mean for the bullet to go as high on him as it did."

Thieves? Yes. Little thieves? Yes. And they get it where the chicken gets the ax? Yes. And the big shots are something else? Yes. And you can't convict a million dollars? Not unless Tuesday is Saturday, neighbor.

What is a jury? Twelve men picked by chance and a couple of lawyers, twelve men good and true or not-so-good, six of one and a half dozen of the other.

A jury? A bundle of twelve fagots, a dozen human sticks light and dark with loves and hates, Protestant, Catholic, Jew, freethinker, merchant, farmer, workingman, thief, wets and drys, union and scab, savers and spenders, tightwads and crapshooters, locked in a room to come out saying Yes in one voice, No in one voice, or else, "Don't ask us what is justice, we agree to disagree," all in one voice.

A jury? Twelve names out of a hat. Twelve picked blindfolded from a city directory or a polling list. The next twelve crossing Main Street, two blocks from the post-office: Odd Fellows, Masons, Knights of Columbus, deacons, poker-players, Democrats, Republicans, Independents, Ku Klux and Anti-Ku Klux, ball fans, chippie chasers, teetotalers, converts and backsliders.

Now you got a jury. Add one judge. Add a few lawyers. Add newspapers, town gossip, "what everybody says." Add witnesses and evidence. Add it all. The jury verdict is guilty not-guilty or agree-to-disagree.

> "Do you solemnly swear before the ever-
> living God that the testimony you
> are about to give in this cause shall
> be the truth, the whole truth, and
> nothing but the truth?"
> "No, I don't. I can tell you what I saw
> and what I heard and I'll swear to
> that by the everliving God but the
> more I study about it the more sure
> I am that nobody but the everliving
> God knows the whole truth and if
> you summoned Christ as a witness in
> this case what He would tell you
> would burn your insides with the
> pity and the mystery of it."

74

What other oaths are wanted now?
You can never make moon poems
for people who never see the moon.
Your moon poems are aimed
at people who look at the moon
and say, "Hello moon, good old moon,
"I knew you wouldn't forget me,
"Throw me a kiss, moon,
"I'll be seeing you, moon."
  And the sun? what of the sun?
  Can you make a sun poem
  For those having soot on the window-sill?
When smoke and smudge and building walls
  Stand between them and the sun
  How can they get to know the sun
And how would they know a sun poem if they
  Met one coming straight at them?
What use for them to hold a hand up against
the sun for the sake of seeing a silhouette
  of the blue frame of the handbones?
  In the slums overshadowed by smokestacks,
  In the tomato cans in the window-sills
  The geraniums have a low weeping song,
  "Not yet have we known the sun,
   not yet have we known the sun,"
  Modulated with a hoping song,
  "Some day we shall meet the sun
 "And gather pieces of the sun into ourselves

"And be no longer stunted,
  no longer runts of the slums."
      And babies? what of the babies?
Can you make baby poems
For those who love special babies
      clean antiseptic babies?
  what of those Red Indian babies
  fresh from the birthing-crotch?
For each of them the mystery-man raised
his right hand toward the sky and called:
"Hey you sun moon stars
            and you winds clouds rain mist,
        "Listen to me! listen!
"The news is another baby belonging
          has come to this earth of ours.
"Make its path smooth so it can reach
            the top of the first hill
            and the second hill.
"And hey you valleys rivers lakes trees grasses
  you make its path smooth so it can reach
            the top of the third hill.
        "And listen you birds of the air,
          you animals of the tall timbers,
          you bugs and creepers,
          you too listen!
"All you of sky earth and air, I ask you, beg you
"Pass this baby on till it climbs up over
          and beyond the fourth hill.
"From then on this child will be strong enough
"To travel on its own and see what is beyond
            those four hills!"

75

Hunger and only hunger changes worlds?
The dictate of the belly
that gnawing under the navel,
this alone is the builder and the pathfinder
sending man into danger and fire
and death by struggle?
    Yes and no, no and yes.
    The strong win against the weak.
    The strong lose against the stronger.
And across the bitter years and the howling winters
    the deathless dream will be the stronger,
    the dream of equity will win.
There are shadows and bones shot with lights
    too strong to be lost.
    Can the wilderness be put behind?
    Shall man always go on dog-eat-dog?
    Who says so?
    The stronger?
    And who is the stronger?
And how long shall the stronger hold on
    as the stronger?
    What will tomorrow write?
    "Of the people by the people for the people?"
What mockers ever wrung a crop from a waiting soil
Or when did cold logic bring forth a child?
"What use is it?" they asked a kite-flying sky gazer
And he wished in return to know, "What use is a baby?"
The dreaming scholars who quested the useless,

who wanted to know merely for the sake of knowing,
they sought and harnessed electrodynamic volts
becoming in time thirty billion horses in one country
hauling with thirty-billion-horse-power
and this is an early glimpse, a dim beginning,
the first hill of a series of hills.

What comes after the spectrum?
With what will the test-tubes be shaken tomorrow?
For what will the acetylene torch and pneumatic chisel be
scrapped?
What will the international partnerships of the world laboratories
track down next, what new fuels, amalgams, alloys, seeds,
cross-breeds, unforeseen short cuts to power?
Whose guess is better than anybody else's on whether the breed
of fire-bringers is run out, whether light rays, death rays,
laugh rays, are now for us only in a dim beginning?
Across the bitter years and the howling winters
the deathless dream will be the stronger
the dream of equity will win.

The record is a scroll of many indecipherable scrawls,
telling the pay of the people for commencing action
toward redress of wrongs too heavy
to be longer borne.

             "No strike is ever lost": an old cry
heard before the strike begins and heard long after, and
"No strike is ever lost": either a thought or an instinct
equivalent to "Give me liberty or give me death."

             On the horizon a cloud no larger than
a man's hand rolls larger and darker when masses of people
begin saying, "Any kind of death is better than this kind
of life."

        The machine world of the insects
        individual spiders engineering exploits
        interwoven colonies of bees and ants
        clouds of grasshopper destroyers
        —they carry lessons and warnings
          they do what they must
          they are beyond argument.

The flowing of the stream clears it of pollution.
The refuse of humanity, the offscourings, the encumberings,
They are who?
They are those who have forgotten work and the price
At which life goes on.
They live in shambles overly foul and in mansions overly
Swept and garnished.
The flowing of the stream clears it of pollution.

77

The bottom of the sea accommodates mountain ranges.
This is how deep the sea is
And the toss and drip of the mystery of the people
And the sting of sea-drip.
In the long catacombs of moss fish linger and move
Hearing the cries of dolphins while they too wander.
This is the depot of lost and unreclaimed baggage,
Colosseums of dead men's bones and the trunks of the
     dead men each with a lock of hair, a ringlet of
     somebody's hair in a locket, and a pack of love
     letters and a deck of cards and a testament and
     leather straps and brass buckles and brass locks
     holding their fasteners on the trunks.

What did Hiamovi, the red man, Chief of
    the Cheyennes, have?
To a great chief at Washington and to a
    chief of peoples across the waters,
    Hiamovi spoke:
"There are birds of many colors—red, blue,
    green, yellow,
Yet it is all one bird.
There are horses of many colors—brown,
    black, yellow, white,
Yet it is all one horse.
So cattle, so all living things, animals,
    flowers, trees.
So men in this land, where once were only
    Indians, are now men of many colors—
    white, black, yellow, red.
Yet all one people.
That this should come to pass was in the
    heart of the Great Mystery.
It is right thus—and everywhere there
    shall be peace."
Thus Hiamovi, out of a tarnished and weather-
    worn heart of old gold, out of a living
    dawn gold.

What is the float of life that goes by us
in certain moods of autumn smoke
when tall trees seem in the possession of phantoms

carrying a scheme of haze
inevitably past changing sunsets
into a moist moonlight
and beyond into a baffling moonset
on a mist horizon?
These devices are made of what color and air?
And how far and in how does man make them himself?
    What is this pool of reverie
    this blur of contemplation
    wherein man is brother to mud and gold
    to bug and bird
    to behemoths and constellations?

In the evening twilight in the skyscraper office
and the hoom hoom of a big steamboat docking
and the auto horns and the corner newsboys
only half heard as far up as sixteen floors
the doctor meditated and spoke: "The rich come afraid to die,
afraid to have their throats looked into, their intestines prod-
ded. It hurts. Their power of resistance is gone. They can't
stand pain. Things go wrong, they come into my office and
ask what is the matter. I have to be careful how I say, 'You
are growing old, that is all, everybody grows old, we all
have to die.' That scares them. They don't want to grow
old. They tell me I must find a way to keep them from
growing old. They don't want to die. They tell me they
will pay me to find a way so they won't have to die." Thus
in the evening twilight, in the hoom hoom and the auto
horns and the corner newsboys only half heard up sixteen
floors.

And he went on:

"I was in a hospital the other day. A man blind thirty-five years
could see again. We walked out together. And up the street
he saw a horse. He asked, 'What is that?' I said, 'It's a horse—
didn't you ever see a horse before?' He answered, 'No, this is
the first time I ever saw a horse.'"

Thus in the evening twilight
in the hoom hoom.

And the doctor went on: "A few weeks ago came a woman saying she had been to a great symphony concert, going out to
walk miles, still hearing the grand crashes of that music,
walking home on air, telling me, 'I went to bed and wept
for three weeks—what is the matter with me?' I had to tell
her, 'Only a slight matter. You will be well again when you
learn to listen to the ticking of the clock.'"

To a lawyer who came saying he had undertaken more financial
reorganizations than there was time for and his nerves were
shot the doctor talked long about worry, gave the lawyer a
box and 100 black beans: "Each morning you drop a bean
in the box and say, 'Worry is in the bean and the bean is in
the box.'"

In the hoom hoom of the big steamboat docking the doctor said,
"Silence is the great gratitude when bad music ends."

79

In paper sacks the customers carry away millions of tons of goods daily except Sunday.

And having used what they carry away in paper sacks they go back daily except Sunday for more millions of tons of useable goods transferred in paper sacks.

And the trade experts look on and call it consumption while the people carrying the paper sacks have a way of alleging, "We have to eat, don't we?"

> And once there was a man who considered how he might make a paper sack song and invent a paper sack dance. In the days of his youth he had worked in the pulp. Joined with other men and machines he had taken logs and cooked a mash and dried and flattened it out and kept flattening it till it was thin as paper and it was paper. And his sister in another mill had watched a machine and tended it; daily except Sunday it spat forth its stint of millions of paper sacks.

And the brother and sister say to each other now, "We have made so many millions of paper sacks we know exactly the feelings and ideas of any one paper sack. One paper sack thinks just what another paper sack thinks. And now when our jobs are gone because bigger and better machines do what we used to do my sister and I say to each other: Hello, old paper sack. And we talk about how we are a couple of paper sacks thrown away and no longer wanted because there is no answer to the question: Why are paper sacks so cheap?

"And we talk on and we decide we are something more than paper sacks. We have a right to live and a right to work and we have a right to say life ought to be good and life is more than paper sacks. And we will go anywhere and listen to any organizers and agitators who come to us saying: We speak to you as people and not as paper sacks."

In Gloversville, New York, a woman daylong made mittens and the faster she made the mittens the more the wages coming in for her and her children.
And her hands became like mittens she said,
And in the winter when she looked out one night
Where the moon lighted a couple of evergreen trees:
"My God! I look at evergreens in the moonlight
and what are they? A pair of mittens.
And what am I myself? Just a mitten.
Only one more mitten, that's all.
My God! if I live a little longer in that mitten factory the whole world will be just a lot of mittens to me
And at last I will be buried in a mitten and on my grave they will put up a mitten as a sign one more mitten is gone."
This was why she listened to the organizer of the glove and mitten workers' union; maybe the union could do something.
She would fight in the union ranks and see if somehow they could save her from seeing two evergreens at night in the moon as just another pair of mitts.

80

Deep in the dusty chattels of the tombs,
Laden with luggage handed them
By departing ghosts saying, "It's yours, all yours,"
They give their ghost imprint to the time they live in.
They are to the people what they are to the sea,
To the harvest moon, to the living grassroots,
To the tides that wash them away babbling to some caretaker,
    "What time is it?   where are we?"

And time, since you ask, time is the story-teller you can't shut
    up, he goes on.
The king, like many a king, was a little coocoo, and hung up a
    challenge. Whoever would tell him a story so long that he
    couldn't stand any more of it would marry his princess
    daughter. Otherwise the story-teller's neck would be blem-
    ished with a gleaming ax-blade. The story-teller began on
    how grain elevators bulging with corn ran for miles while
    the locusts spread out many more miles and there was only
    one point of entry and egress for the crawling hordes of
    slithering locusts, only one place for a locust to go in and
    out. And one locust went in and brought out a grain of corn
    and another locust went in and brought out another grain
    of corn. And another locust went in and brought out an-
    other grain of corn. And another locust went in and brought
    out another grain of corn. And so on and so on till the king
    saw what he had let himself in for and speaking in the royal
    tone customary to kings he told the story-teller, "You win,

the girl is yours." And this was back in the old days when
kings were kings and wore crowns and had crown jewels.
Time? The story-teller you can't shut up, he goes on.

"Time is blind; man stupid."
Thus one of the cynics.
"Time is relentless; man shrewd."
Thus one of the hopefuls.
Time passes; man laughs at it.
The sun-dial was one laugh.
The wrist-watch is another.
"Time? I can't stop it but I
can measure it."

81

Chicago seems all fox and swine,
Dreams interfused with smut, dung, hunger.
Yet Chicago is not all belly and mouth and
    overwrought sex and lies and greed
    and snobs.
Chicago has something over and beyond.
Sometime the seeds and cross-fertilizations
    now moving in Chicago may inaugurate
    a crossroads of great gladness.
The same goes for Omaha and points west,
    for Buffalo and points east.

Out of the shopping crowds at State and Madison, hot with bun-
    dles and bargains,
A humpty-dumpty runt of a man dived at high noon into a
    forest of rubbernecks craning at a skywriting plane telling
    you what cigarette to smoke next, what cigarette to buy,
And he came up to say there was too much quick thinking and
    he would offer a little slow thinking:
"From the museum mummies I came to these ghosts swirling
    around State and Madison, Forty-second and Fifth Avenue,
    and about all I learned was this, you can write it on a thumb-
    nail:
"There is a dead past and a blank future and the same humanity
    is in each and it's all ham and eggs, dog eat dog, the tough-
    est guts have their way, and they kill and kill to see who'll
    get the most marbles, the most cocoanuts, the most little em-
    bossed pieces of paper."

And then he went on, wiping his chin with four fingers and a thumb, screwing his eyes to a thin slit, and correcting himself:

"I take that back. Write it off as a loss. If the big arch of the sky were paper and the violet depths of the sea were ink, I could never live long enough to write the dreams of man and the dynamic drive of those dreams.

"Who and what is man? He is Atlas and Thor and Yankee Doodle, an eagle, a lion, a rooster, a bear that walks like a man, an elephant, a moon-face, David and Goliath, Paul Bunyan and the Flying Dutchman, Shakespeare, Lincoln and Christ, the Equator and the Arctic Poles, holding in one hand the Bank of England and the Roman Catholic Church, in the other the Red Army and the Standard Oil Company, holding in easy reach the dogs of war and the doves of peace, the tigers of wrath and the horses of instruction.

"Let me sell you my dreams. Take these dreams for whatever you want to pay me. You shall never be tired till the sea is tired. You shall never go weary till the land and the wind go weary. You will be hard as nails, soft as blue fog.

"Man is born with rainbows in his heart and you'll never read him unless you consider rainbows. He is a trouble shooter with big promises. He trades the Oklahoma roan mustang for a tub in the sky with wings falling falling in Alaska. Hard as a rock his head is an egg and ponders ponders. He is a phantasmagoria of crimson dawns and what it takes to build his dreams."

So the finish. He ceased from wiping his chin with four fingers and a thumb, ceased from screwing his eyes to a thin slit, ceased correcting himself.

208

Then he vanished. In a wreath of blue smoke from a panatella seegar he was gone, a scholar, a clown, and a dreambook seller who had said enough for one day.

Turning a corner he talked to himself about the dust of the knuckles of his great-grandfathers, how they once were hard as nails and could pick a vest-button with a bullet, and how his own little knuckles sometime would shiver into fine dust and how he wanted snowdrifts piled over him and the inscription: HERE NO ONE LIES BURIED.

82

I pledge my allegiance,
say the munitions makers and the international bankers,
I pledge my allegiance to this flag, that flag,
any flag at all, of any country anywhere
paying its bills and meeting interest on loans,
one and indivisible,
coming through with cash in payment as stipulated
with liberty and justice for all,
say the munitions makers and the international bankers.

> "Your million dollars, if you will pardon me,"
> said a polite shrimp, "came one of three
> ways. First, if you will pardon me, you
> took it somehow as profits within the law
> belonging to you, unless, second, you have
> it as a gift or bequest handed to you with-
> out your working for it, or unless, if you
> will pardon me, third and last, you took
> it, outside the law and yet beyond the
> reach of the law, as belonging to you
> rather than whoever had it before you
> got it from them."

What good is rain on a hard and sour soil?
Why put a driller and seeder
where the top soil is blown away?
Why put your headlights on in bright noon?
Why do favors where you know you get no thanks?

Some have their finger nails pinked
a regular shade, according to custom.
Some, wearing pearls, have their finger-nails
tinted, enameled and polished
to match the precise color of their pearls.
Those with oyster pearls shade to a crystal,
others are touched with desert grey, sea green.
And cosmetics volume last year was over a billion.

83

Who can make a poem of the depths of weariness
bringing meaning to those never in the depths?
    Those who order what they please
    when they choose to have it—
    can they understand the many down under
who come home to their wives and children at night
and night after night as yet too brave and unbroken
    to say, "I ache all over"?
    How can a poem deal with production cost
    and leave out definite misery paying
a permanent price in shattered health and early old age?
    When will the efficiency engineers and the poets
    get together on a program?
Will that be a cold day? will that be a special hour?
    Will somebody be coocoo then?
    And if so, who?
    And what does the Christian Bible say?
And the Mohammedan Koran and Confucius and the Shintoists
    and the Encyclicals of the Popes?
    Will somebody be coocoo then?
    And if so, who??

84

In the chain store or the independent it is the people meeting
the people: "Would you like to be waited on? Could I wait
on you? Could I be of assistance? Is there something you
would like? Is there something for you? Could I help you?
Anything I can help you to? What will yours be? What
can I get for you? What would you like? Is there something?"

The rodeo hoss wrangler, the airplane stunter,
the living cannonball shot from a gun,
the animal tamer amid paws and fangs—
they use up their luck ahead of time,
they bet their necks and earn a living:
they play fair with their seen galleries
the same as lone hunters and explorers
aim to please unseen acres of fine faces,
aim to tell about it later maybe
if a public cares to hear.

In this corner the spotlighted challenger,
in this corner the world's heavyweight champ
along with camera boys grinding,
lads at the mikes giving round by round,
they aim to please,
to put it over big
for the fish on the spot,
for the many more fish beyond,
one sports writer quizzing another,

"How many of the fish are here?
"What's your guess?"

The world series pitcher pets his arm,
prays he won't get a glass arm:
he too strives to please:
he would like to put smoke on the ball
and throw a hitless game:
when the big-boy home-run hitter
has an off day and fans the air,
at the umpire's cry "three strikes"
he may hear from the bleachers,
"Take the big bum out."

One movie star arches her eyebrows
and refers to "my public."
One soda-jerker arches his eyebrows,
curves malt-milk from shaker to glass
and speaks of "my public."
The dance marathon winning couple
bow sleepy thanks to their public.
The fire department ladder truck driver
sees his public at a standstill
on the sidewalk curbs.
The going-going-gone jewelry auctioneer
plays to another public.
And at every street intersection
these publics intersect.

Ringmasters in top hats, clowns on mules,
circus riders in spangles,

little ladies doing somersaults on horses,
      acrobat families in pink tights
      sliding their own human toboggans—
the peanut, popcorn, and red lemonade sellers
they feel their crowds and read crowd moods.

"I know why I lost my crowd tonight,"
  said a flame of an actor.
"I never can do anything with them
  unless I love them."

The breezes of surface change blow lightly.
The people take what comes, hold on, let go.
      The high wheel bicycle was a whiz.
      Eskimo pie raked in a lot of jack.
      The tom thumb golf courses had a run.
      Yo yo charmed till yo yo checked out.
      The tree sitters climbed up, came down.
Sideburns, galways, handlebar mustaches, full beards,
they flitted away on winds whistling,
      "Where are the snows of yesteryear?"
meaning snow and stage-snow, the phony and the real
      gone to the second-hand bins, the rummage sales,
      the Salvation Army wagons.

      Stronger winds blow slow.
      Trial balloons are sent up.
      The public says yes, says no.
      The whim of the public rides.
      A hoarse cry carves events.

The platoon of police in uniform,
the drum-major with his baton
and a gold ball high in the air,
The silver cornet band, the fife-and-drum corps,
the Knights of Pythias in plume and gilt braid,
the speakers of the day with mounted escorts,
the fire department, the Odd Fellows, the Woodmen,
the civilian cohorts following the local militia,
American Legion, Veterans of Foreign Wars,
they march between sidewalks
heavy with a human heave,
heavy with vox populi.

"Me too, count me in.
"I want to belong.
"I do what's regular.
"I'll sign up.
"A trial package can't hurt me.
"Here's my name and dues.
"I'll try anything once."
This is the tune of today's razzle-dazzle.
Tomorrow the tune is never quite the same.
Tomorrow's children have it *their* own way.

When the yes-men no longer yes
or the no-men shift their no
anything is in the cards.

Ask the public relations counsel.
He is a shortstop and a scavenger
smooth as a big league umpire

cool as a veteran horse race jockey
cool as a cube of cucumber on ice.
He will tell you there is a public
and this public has many relations
and you can't have too much counsel
when you're trying to handle it.
    Our ghost writers will ghost for you:
    they write it, you hand it out
    or you speak the speech written for you
    and nobody knows but the ghost
    and the ghost is paid
    for helping you with your public.

The cheer leader struts his stuff,
wigwags the swaying grand stand,
throws himself into alphabetical shapes
trying to orchestrate his crowd:
the fads and fashions innovators,
the halitosis and body odor frighteners,
the skin and complexion fixers,
the cigarette ads lying about relative values.
the nazi imitators, the fascisti imitators,
the ku klux klan and the konklave's wizard,
the makers of regalia, insignia, masks,
hoods, hats, nightshirts, skull-and-crossbones,
the spellbinder calling on all true patriots,
the soapboxer pleading for the proletariat,
the out-of-works marching marching
with demands and banners, "why? why?"
the strike leader telling why the men walked out,

the million-dollar-national-sales-campaign director,
the headache copy writer groping for one new idea,
the drive organizers planning their hoorah,
the neighborhood captains of tens and twenties,
the best-seller authors, the by-line correspondents,
the President at the White House microphone,
the Senators, Congressmen, spokesmen, at microphones—
   Each and all have a target.
   Each one aims for the ping ping
   the bling bling of a sharpshooter.
      Here is a moving colossal show,
   a vast dazzling aggregation of stars and hams
   selling things, selling ideas, selling faiths,
   selling air, slogans, passions, selling history.
      The target is who and what?
         The people, yes—
      sold and sold again
      for losses and regrets,
      for gains, for slow advances,
      for a dignity of deepening roots.

85

One memorial stone reads:
"We, near whose bones you stand, were Iroquois.
The wide land which is now yours, was ours.
Friendly hands have given us back enough for a tomb."

Breeds run out
and shining names
no longer shine.
Tribes, clans, nations, have their hour,
Hang up their records and leave.
Yet who could chisel on a gravestone:
"Here lies John Doe," or,
"Here rest the mortal remains of Richard Roe"
And then step back and read the legend and say,
"Can this be so when I myself am John Doe,
when I myself am Richard Roe"?

pack up your bundle now and go
be a seeker among voices and faces
on main street in a bus station at a union depot
this generation of eaters sleepers lovers toilers
flowing out of the last one now buried
flowing into the next one now unborn
short of cash and wondering where to?   what next?
jobs bosses paydays want-ads groceries soap
board and clothes and a corner to sleep in
just enough to get by
when its lamplighting time in the valley
where is my wandering boy tonight

in the beautiful isle of somewhere
the latest extra and another ax murder
he's forgotten by the girl he can't forget
she lives in a mansion of aching hearts
tickets? where to? round trip or one way?
room rent coffee and doughnuts maybe a movie
suit-cases packsacks bandannas
names saved and kept careful
you mustn't lose the address
and what'll be your telephone number?
give me something to remember you by
be my easy rider
kiss me once before you go a long one
flash eyes testaments in a rush
underhums of plain love with rye bread sandwiches
and grief and laughter: where to? what next?

86

The people, yes, the people,
Until the people are taken care of one way or another,
Until the people are solved somehow for the day and hour,
Until then one hears "Yes but the people what about the people?"
Sometimes as though the people is a child to be pleased or fed
Or again a hoodlum you have to be tough with
And seldom as though the people is a caldron and a reservoir
Of the human reserves that shape history,
The river of welcome wherein the broken First Families fade,
The great pool wherein wornout breeds and clans drop for re-
    storative silence.

    Fire, chaos, shadows,
Events trickling from a thin line of flame
On into cries and combustions never expected:
The people have the element of surprise.
    Where are the kings today?
What has become of their solid and fastened thrones?
Who are the temporary puppets holding sway while anything,
    "God only knows what," waits around a corner, sits in the
        shadows and holds an ax, waiting for the appointed
        hour?

    "The czar has eight million men with guns and bayonets.
    "Nothing can happen to the czar.
    "The czar is the voice of God and shall live forever.
    "Turn and look at the forest of steel and cannon
    "Where the czar is guarded by eight million soldiers.
    "Nothing can happen to the czar."

They said that for years and in the summer of 1914
In the Year of Our Lord Nineteen Hundred and Fourteen
As a portent and an assurance they said with owl faces:
    "Nothing can happen to the czar."
Yet the czar and his bodyguard of eight million vanished
And the czar stood in a cellar before a little firing squad
And the command of fire was given
And the czar stepped into regions of mist and ice
The czar travelled into an ethereal uncharted siberia
While two kaisers also vanished from thrones
Ancient and established in blood and iron—
Two kaisers backed by ten million bayonets
Had their crowns in a gutter, their palaces mobbed.
    In fire, chaos, shadows,
In hurricanes beyond foretelling of probabilities,
In the shove and whirl of unforeseen combustions
    The people, yes, the people,
Move eternally in the elements of surprise,
Changing from hammer to bayonet and back to hammer,
The hallelujah chorus forever shifting its star soloists.

87

The people learn, unlearn, learn,
a builder, a wrecker, a builder again,
a juggler of shifting puppets.
  In so few eyeblinks
   In transition lightning streaks,
the people protect midgets into giants,
the people shrink titans into dwarfs.

   Faiths blow on the winds
   and become shibboleths
   and deep growths
   with men ready to die
for a living word on the tongue,
for a light alive in the bones,
for dreams fluttering in the wrists.

For liberty and authority they die
though one is fire and the other water
and the balances of freedom and discipline
are a moving target with changing decoys.

Revolt and terror pay a price.
Order and law have a cost.
What is this double use of fire and water?
Where are the rulers who know this riddle?
On the fingers of one hand you can number them.
How often has a governor of the people first
  learned to govern himself?

The free man willing to pay and struggle and die
    for the freedom for himself and others
Knowing how far to subject himself to discipline
    and obedience for the sake of an ordered so-
    ciety free from tyrants, exploiters and
    legalized frauds—
This free man is a rare bird and when you meet
    him take a good look at him and try
    to figure him out because
Some day when the United States of the Earth
    gets going and runs smooth and pretty there
    will be more of him than we have now.

88

The response of wild birds
to a home on the way,
a stopping place of rest,
this and the wish of a child
to eat the moon
as a golden ginger cookie—
this is in the songs of the people.

The clods of the earth hold place
close to the whir of yellow hummingbird wings
and they divide into those hard of hearing
and those whose ears pick off
a smooth hush with a little wind whimper across it
and then again only the smooth hush.

What are these dialects deep under the bones
whereby the people of ages and races far apart
reach out and say the same clay is in all,
bringing out men whose eyes
search the earth and see no aliens anywhere,
pronouncing across the barriers the peculiar word:
    "Brother"?

Washing his shirt in a jungle near Omaha,
warming his java under a C.B.&Q. bridge,
a hobo mumbled to himself a mumbling poem
and said it was an outline of history
and you could take it or leave it,

you could ride the rods or hunt an empty
and he would mumble:
> "A hammering, a neverending hammering goes on.
> Suns and moons by platoons batter down
> the shovels and the clamps
> of other suns and moons.
> "By platoons always by platoons under a hammering,
> the cries of the tongs go kling klong
> to the bong bong of the hammers."

The bulls took him in.
The bulls gathered him.
In the lockup he thought it over.
In the cooler he was not so hot,
They said, and further they said,
He was nuts, he was dopey from white mule.
> Yet he kept on with his mumbling
> of the shovels and the clamps,
> of the tongs going kling klong
> and the bong bong of the hammers,
> of history and its awful anvils.

> "Listen," he cried,
"Kling klong go the mighty hammers,
kling klong on a mighty anvil,
steel on steel they clash and weld,
how long can you last? how long?
goes the clamor of the hammer and the anvil,
how long? goes the steel kling klong:
the gunmetal blue gives it and takes it:

226

in the fire and the pounding:
the hard old answer goes:
    let the works go on:
I will last a long time: yet a long time."

    A fly-by-night house, a shanty,
a ramshackle hut of tarpaper, tin cans,
body by fisher, frames from flivvers,
a shelter from rain and wind,
the home of a homeseeker having an alibi,
why did two hungers move across his face?
    One: when do we eat?
    The other: What is worth looking at?
              what is worth listening to?
              why do we live?
              when is a homeseeker
                    just one more trespasser?
              and what is worth dying for?

89

Marshall Field the First was spick and span while alive
and wishing to be well kept and properly groomed
in the long afterward
he stipulated in a clause of his will
a fund of $25,000 be set aside and its income be devoted
to the upkeep of his tomb.

The country editor of Stoughton, Wisconsin,
was not so careful, less spick and span.
He left orders to the typesetters and they obeyed him.
His obituary read: "Charlie Cross is dead."
And that was all.
John Eastman died leaving the Chicago Journal to four men,
to four old friends who knew how to get out the paper.
And to make sure the obsequies would be correct and decent
he instructed in his last will and testament:
"Let no words of praise be spoken at my funeral."

What about that Chinese poet
traveling on a cart
with a jug of wine,
a shovel and a grave-digger?
Each morning as they started
he told the grave-digger:
"Bury me when I am dead—
anywhere, anytime."
He was afraid of a fancy funeral.
What did he have?
He would be covered down like any coolie
"anywhere, anytime," no music, no flowers.

What about that radio operator in the North Atlantic
on a stormlashed sinking Scandinavian ship
laughing the wireless message:
"God pity the poor sailors on a night like this"
adding word they were heading for Davy Jones' locker
and adding further:
"This is no night to be out without an umbrella!"
    What about him?
    And what did he have?
He went to a sea-tomb laughing an epitaph:
    "This is no night to be out without an umbrella."

Who was that professor at the University of Wisconsin work-
    ing out a butter-fat milk tester
Good for a million dollars if he wanted a patent with sales and
    royalties
And he whistled softly and in dulcet tone: What in God's name
    do I want with a million dollars?
Whistling as though instead of his owning the million it would
    own him.

    Who was that South Dakota Norwegian who
        went to Siberia and brought back
    Wheat grains pushing the North American wheat
        area hundreds of miles northward?
    He could have had a million dollars and took
        instead a million thanks.

    Why did the two high wizards of applied
        electrodynamics say

All they wanted was board and clothes and time
    to think things over?
Why did they go along so careless about dollars,
    so forgetful about millions,
Letting others organize and gather the shekels
    and progress from boom to crash to boom
    to crash?
Why is the Schenectady hunchback dwarf one
    of the saints in shirtsleeves?
And why did the deaf mechanic in Orange, New
    Jersey, forget to eat unless his wife called
    him,
And why did he die saying: What is electricity?
    we don't know. What is heat? we don't know.
    We are beginners. "Look at the moon—it
    winks at the ignorance of the world."

What of the Wright boys in Dayton? Just around the corner
they had a shop and did a bicycle business—and they wanted
to fly for the sake of flying.

They were Man the Seeker, Man on a Quest. Money was their
last thought, their final absent-minded idea.

They threw out a lot of old mistaken measurements and figured
new ones that stood up when they took off and held the air
and steered a course. They proved "the faster you go the
less power you need."

One of them died and was laid away under blossoms dropped
from zooming planes. The other lived on to meditate: what
is *attraction?* when will we learn *why* things go when they
go?   what and where is the power?

230

Why is raggedy Johnny Appleseed half-man half-myth? From old cider mills he filled his sacks with apple-seeds and out of his plantings came orchards in Ohio and Indiana. "God ordained me a sower to sow that others might reap." Why will they remember the earthly shadow of Johnny with bronze figures tomorrow in Ohio and Indiana?

> Was it true that Van Gogh cut off
> one of his ears
> and gave it to a daughter
> of the streets,
> to one who had pleasured him?
> And if he did what did he mean by it?
> And who could guess what Van Gogh
> had in mind if anything in particular?
> > In and out by thousands they went
> > to see the Van Gogh exhibit
> > of paintings touring America,
> > in and out by thousands
> > finding the color and line
> > of a plain strange personality,
> > something dear and rich
> > out of the umber of the earth.
> Somewhere in what he flung from his brush
> > was a missing ear
> > and why it might be missed
> > and a blunt gesture,
> > "What of it?"

Why did the St. Louis Mirror editor name as his favorite Shakespeare line: "I myself am but indifferent honest"? and how

did he mean it when in an owl-car dawn, ending a long
night of talk, he blurted to a poet, "God damn it, I tell you
there are no *bad* people"?

Who was the St. Louis mathematician who figured it cost an
average of $37,000 to kill each soldier killed in the World
War?
He figured too on a way of offering, in case of war, $1,000, one
grand, to every deserting soldier.
Each army, the idea ran, would buy off the other before the war
could get started.

Who was that Pittsburgh Scotchman terrorized by having a
quarter billion dollars?
Why did he give it away before he died as though he could
never take it away with him?
Who was the Chicago Jew who threw millions of dollars into
Negro schools of the South?
Why did he once tell another Jew, "I'm ashamed to have so
much money"?

"There are no pockets in the shroud" may be carried farther:
"The dead hold in their clenched hands only that which they
have given away."

Who was that Roman: "I am a man and nothing on legs and
human is a stranger to me"?
He could have met the first Negro who sang: "When you see
me laughing I'm laughing to keep from crying."

Did he give them a high and roaring laughter when he had his
throne moved out into the sea,

232

When he sat in his sea-set throne and commanded the tide: "Go
   back! go back! it is I, King Knute who tell you so and I am
   putting you to this test because a circle of my advisers have
   told me over and again that I am beyond other plain people,
   I am made of no common clay and what I say goes and even
   the ocean will obey me and do what I say and therefore I
   give you the order to Go back! go back! and don't dare
   bring your stink of seawrack and salt water even to the
   footstool of this royal throne of mine"?
Did he give them a high and roaring laughter as the tide slowly
   and inexorably rose over his footstool, to his knees, to his
   navel, to his neck,
When he rose, plunged and swam ashore and told them to let
   the throne be washed out to join the flotsam and jetsam of
   the immemorial sea?

Who was the young Nicodemus in Chicago so early in the twentieth century falling heir to a million dollars and writing a
   pamphlet of public inquiry titled The Confessions of a
   Drone and having one luminous and quivering question to
   ask:
Why was this money wished on me merely because I was born
   where I couldn't help being born so that I don't have to
   work while a lot of people work for me and I can follow
   the races, yacht, play horse polo, chase if I so choose any
   little international chippie that takes my eye, eat nightin-
   gale tongues, buy sea islands or herds of elephants or trained
   fleas, or go to Zanzibar, to Timbuctoo, to the mountains of
   the moon, and never work an hour or a day and when I
   come back I find a lot of people working for me because I
   was born where I couldn't help being born?

90

The big fish eat the little fish,
the little fish eat shrimps
and the shrimps eat mud.
You don't know enough to come in when it rains.
You don't know beans when the bag is open.
You don't know enough to pound sand in a rat hole.
All I know is what I hear.
All I know is what I read in the papers.
All I know you can put in a thimble.
All I know I keep forgetting.

We have to eat, don't we?
You can't eat promises, can you?
You can't eat the Constitution, can you?
I can eat crow but I don't hanker after it.
Don't quarrel with your bread and butter.
Some curse the hand that feeds them.
Many kiss the hands they wish to see cut off.
You can't rob a naked man of his clothes.
He that makes himself an ass, men will ride him,
Stand like a good mule and you're soon harnessed.

Be not rash with thy mouth.
Praise no man before his death,
When pups bark old dogs go along doing whatever
it was they were doing.
He who blackens others does not whiten himself.
The camel has his plans, the camel driver his plans.

The horse thinks one thing, he who saddles him another.
    Ask me no questions and I tell you no lies.
    The best witness is a written paper.
    Liars should have good memories.
    Some liars get monotonous.
    Hearsay is half lies.
    To say nothing is to say yes.
    Hold your tongue one second and
    a bundle of trouble is held off.
    Be careful what you say or
    you go out of the door
    and meet yourself coming in.
Hunger and cold deliver a man to his enemy.
    Hunger says to hell with the law.
    The empty belly instructs the tongue.
    Want changes men into wild animals.
Unless you say eat the hungry belly can't
    hear you.

91

Who were those editors picking the most
detestable word in the English language
and deciding the one word just a little
worse than any other you can think of
is "Exclusive"?

The doorbells were many and the approaches screened and the
corners hushed in the care of frozen-faced butlers and foot-
men in livery, London trained, chauffeurs, cooks, maids,
twenty-two when counted, for personal service in the Lake
Shore Drive apartments overlooking one blue of water meeting another blue of skyline.

And one young man yawned over his real estate and securities,
his Chicago and Manhattan skyscrapers, his silk mills in
France, his woolen mills in Scotland, his cotton mills north
and south in the States, yawned over the caretakers and
trustees sober and dependable in custody of what had grown
since he was a baby to whom accrued from a dying father
an estate beyond one hundred millions, one blue of water
meeting another blue of skyline then as now. Across the dust
and roar of Halsted Street he rode one afternoon into the
seething jungles and slums of the West Side, to yawn and
smile, "This is No-man's land to me," never to go back, to
sense it as a dull and alien rabble, a polyglot of panhandlers
mooching pig-stickers, structural ironworkers after a day
with rivets and bolts lifting schooners of beer to laugh,
"Here every man is as good as the next one and for the
matter of that a little better."

236

To a Long Island Sound country mansion he fled and in a scarlet
English hunting coat shot pheasants by the hundreds with
retainers loading the guns for him and his guests; to Buck-
ingham Palace he flitted, to the African gold coast, to the
Riviera, to Biarritz, to nowhere among multiplied nothings,
from wife to wife and tweedledum to tweedledee, in car,
yacht and plane fleeing from No-man's land, with a personal
service staff of twenty-two when counted, and always from
the Lake Shore Drive one blue of water meeting another
blue of skyline.

And who are these others?
Why, they are the three tailors of Tooley Street, signing themselves, "We, the people,"
Having an audacity easier to look at than three others, namely,
one prime minister, one banker, one munitions maker, in
the name of the people letting loose a war.
These others, you may have read, are "the great unwashed," "the
hoi polloi," they are indicated with gestures:
"The rabble," "the peepul," "the mob with its herd instinct in its
wild stampede," "the irresponsible ragtag and bobtail"—
Can they also be the multitude fed by a miracle on loaves and
fishes, les misérables in a pit, in a policed abyss of want?
Was it this same miscellany heard the Sermon on the Mount, the
Gettysburg Speech, the Armistice Day news when confetti
dotted the window-sills and white paper blew in snowdrifts
on the city streets?
And in the Gettysburg speech was it written, "of the peepul, by
the peepul, and for the peepul"?

237

When they gather the voices and prints from above what most
    often do they hear and read?
They are told to go north and south at once, for liberty, to go
    east and west at once, for liberty.
The advice is pounded in their ears, "Go up, go down, stand
    where you are, for liberty."
In one ear comes the clamor, "You are damned if you do," in
    the other ear, "You are damned if you don't."
And when liberty is all washed up the dictators say:
    "You are the greatest people on earth and we shall shoot
        only as many of you as necessary."

        Out of this mass are shaped
    Armies, navies, work gangs, wrecking crews.
        Here are the roars to shake walls
        and set roofs shuddering,
    Hecklers ready with hoots, howls, boos, meeouw,
    Bronx cheers, the razzberry, the bum's rush,
    Straw hats by thousands thrown from the bleachers,
    Pop bottles by hundreds aimed at an umpire,
    The units of the bargain sale crush, the subway jam,
    The office building emptying its rush hour stream,
    The millions at radio sets for an earful,
    The millions turning newspaper pages for an eyeful:
        This is the source and the headwater
    Of tomorrow's Niagara of action, monotony, action,
        rapids, plungers, whirlpool and mist
        of the people and by the people,
        a long street and a vast field of faces,
        faces across an immeasurable mural,

faces shifting on an incalculable panel,
touched and dented with line and contrast,
potatoes winking at cherry blossoms,
roses here and ashes of roses there,
thornapple branches hung with redhaws,
hickory side by side with moss violets,
the mangelwurzer elbowing the orchid.

Here is a huggermugger becoming
a cloud of witnesses, a juggernaut,
the Mississippi asking the peaks of the Rockies,
    "How goes it?"
a hallelujah chorus forever changing its star soloists,
    taking pyramid, pagoda and skyscraper in its stride,
    having survival elements and gifts in perpetuity,
    requiring neither funeral march, memorial nor epitaph.
    Why should the continuing generations
who replenish themselves in the everliving earth
need any tall symbol set up to be gazed at
as a sign they are gone, past, through,
when they are here yet,
so massively and chorally here yet
in a multitudinous trampling
of shoes and wheels, hands and tools, having heard:
    "The voice of the people is the voice of God,"
having heard, "Be ye comforted for your dreams shall come true
    on earth by your own works,"
having heard, "Ye shall know the truth and the truth shall make
    you free."

The wheel turns.
The wheel comes to a standstill.
The wheel waits.
The wheel turns.

"Something began me
and it had no beginning:
something will end me
and it has no end."

The people is a long shadow
trembling around the earth,
stepping out of fog gray into smoke red
and back from smoke red into fog gray
and lost on parallels and meridians
learning by shock and wrangling,
by heartbreak so often and loneliness so raw
the laugh comes at least half true,
"My heart was made to be broken."

"Man will never write,"
they said before the alphabet came
and man at last began to write.
"Man will never fly,"
they said before the planes and blimps
zoomed and purred in arcs
winding their circles around the globe.

"Man will never make the United States of Europe
nor later yet the United States of the World,
"No, you are going too far when you talk about one

world flag for the great Family of Nations,"
they say that now.

And man the stumbler and finder, goes on,
    man the dreamer of deep dreams,
    man the shaper and maker,
    man the answerer.
The first wheel maker saw a wheel, carried
in his head a wheel, and one day found his
hands shaping a wheel, the first wheel.
The first wagon makers saw a wagon, joined
their hands and out of air, out of what
had lived in their minds, made the first
wagon.
One by one man alone and man joined
has made things with his hands
beginning in the fog wisp of a dim imagining
resulting in a tool, a plan, a working model,
    bones joined to breath being alive
in wheels within wheels, ignition, power,
transmission, reciprocals, beyond man alone,
alive only with man joined.
                Where to? what next?

Man the toolmaker, tooluser,
son of the burning quests
fixed with roaming forearms,
hands attached to the forearms,
fingers put on those hands,
a thumb to face any finger—

hands cunning with knives, leather, wood,
    hands for twisting, weaving, shaping—
Man the flint grinder, iron and bronze welder,
    smoothing mud into hut walls,
    smoothing reinforced concrete into
    bridges, breakwaters, office buildings—
two hands projected into vast claws, giant hammers,
    into diggers, haulers, lifters.
The clamps of the big steam shovel? man's two hands:
the motor hurling man into high air? man's two hands:
    the screws of his skulled head
    joining the screws of his hands,
pink convolutions transmitting to white knuckles
    waves, signals, buttons, sparks—
    man with hands for loving and strangling,
    man with the open palm of living handshakes,
man with the closed nails of the fist of combat—
    these hands of man—where to? what next?

92

The breathing of the earth
may be heard along with
the music of the sea
in their joined belongings.

Consider the ears of a donkey
and the varied languages entering them.
Study the deep-sea squid
and see how he does only what he has to,
how the wild ducks of autumn
come flying in a shifting overhead scroll,
how rats earn a living and survive
and pass on their tough germ plasms
to children who can live where others die.
Mink are spotlessly clean for special reasons.
The face of a goat has profound contemplations.
Only a fish can do the autobiography of a fish.

93

An aster, a farewell-summer flower, stays long in the last fall weeks,

Lingers in fence corners where others have shivered and departed.

The whites have mentioned it as the last-rose-of-summer, the red man saying, "It-brings-the-frost."

Late in the morning and only when sun-warmed does the flower-of-an-hour, the good-night-at-noon, open a while and then close its blossoms.

Even in the noon sun the scarlet pimpernel may shut its petals, as a storm sign, earning its ancient name of wink-a-peep and sometimes called the poor-man's-weather-glass.

John-go-to-bed-at-noon is the goat's beard plant shutting itself at twelve o'clock and showing again only when the next day's sun is out.

One looped vine of the hop-growers is a kiss-me-quick and more than one red flower blooming in rock corners is a love-lies-bleeding or a look-up-and-kiss-me.

The saskatoon is a shadblow looming white in the spring weeks when the shad are up the rivers and spawning,

And hanging its branches with the June berry, the Indian cherry, it is still the saskatoon fed by the melted snows of chinooks.

The toadflax, the ox-eye daisy, the pussy willow, rabbit bells, buffalo clover, swamp candles and wafer ash,

These with the windrose and the rockrose, lady slippers, loose-strife, thornapples, dragon's blood, old man's flannel,

And the horse gentian, dog laurel, cat tails, snakeroot, spiderwort,

pig weed, sow thistle, skunk cabbage, goose grass, moonseed,
    poison hemlock,
These with the names on names between horse radish and the
    autumn-flowering orchid of a lavish harvest moon—
These are a few of the names clocked and pronounced by the
    people in the moving of the earth from season to season.

The red and white men traded plants and words back and forth.
The Shawnee haw and the Choctaw root, the paw paw, the
    potato, the cohosh and your choice of the yellow puccoon
    or white,
A cork elm or a western buckthorn or a burning bush, each a
    wahoo and all of the wahoo family
These from the tongues of name givers, from a restless name
    changer, the people.

94

The sea only knows the bottom of the ship.
One grain of wheat holds all the stars.
The bosoms of the wise are the tombs of secrets.
When you must, walk as if on egg shells.
It looks good but is it foolproof?
Only a poor fisherman curses the river he fishes in.
I can read your writing but I can't read your mind.
        Threatened men live long.
        The glad hand became the icy mitt.
Applause is the beginning of abuse.
If born to be hanged you shall never be drowned.
Life without a friend is death without a witness.
        Sleep is the image of death.
Six feet of earth make us all of one size.
The oldest man that ever lived died at last.
The turnip looked big till the pumpkin walked in.
The dime looked different when the dollar arrived.
        Who said you are the superintendent?
        Spit on your hands and go to work.
Three generations from shirtsleeves to shirtsleeves.
We won't see it but our children will.

        Everything is in the books.
        Too many books overload the mind.
        Who knows the answers?
        Step by step one goes far.
The greatest cunning is to have none at all.
        Sow wind and you reap whirlwind.
A hundred years is not much but never is a long while.

246

A good blacksmith likes a snootful of smoke.
Fire is a good servant and a bad master.
You can fight fire with fire.
The fireborn are at home in fire.

The stars make no noise.
You can't hinder the wind from blowing.
Who could live without hope?

95

Sayings, sentences, what of them?
Flashes, lullabies, are they worth remembering?
On the babbling tongues of the people have these been kept.
In the basic mulch of human culture are these grown.
Along with myths of rainbow gold where you shovel all you
    want and take it away,
Along with hopes of a promised land, a homestead farm, and a
    stake in the country,
Along with prayers for a steady job, a chicken in the pot and
    two cars in the garage, the life insurance paid, and a home
    your own.

    In sudden flash and in massive chaos
    the tunes and cries of the people
    rise in the scripts of Bach and Moussorgsky.
The people handle the food you eat, the clothes you wear,
        and stick by stick and stone by stone
        the houses you live in, roof and walls,
        and wheel by wheel, tire by tire,
        part by part your assembled car,
and the box car loadings of long and short hauls.

Those who have nothing stand in two pressures.
Either what they once had was taken away
Or they never had more than subsistence.
Long ago an easy category was provided for them:
    "They live from hand to mouth,"
Having the name of horny-handed sons of toil.
From these hands howsoever horny, from these sons,

Pours a living cargo of overwhelming plenty
From land and mill into the world markets.
  Their pay for this is what is handed them.
Or they take no pay at all if the labor market is glutted,
Losing out on pay if the word is: "NO HANDS WANTED
         next month maybe
         next year maybe
         the works start."

96

Big oil tanks squat next the railroad.
The shanties of the poor wear cinder coats.
The red and blue lights signal.
The control board tells the story.
Lights go on and off on a map.
Each light is a train gone by
Or a train soon heaving in.

    The big chutes grow cold.
    They stack up shadows.
    Their humps hold iron ore.
    This gang works hard.
    Some faces light up to hear:
    "We work today—
      what do you know about that?"

97

Somebody has to make the tubs and pails.
Not yet do the tubs and pails grow on trees
    and all you do is pick 'em.
For tubs and pails we go first to the timber cruisers, to the log-
    gers, hewers, sawyers, choppers, peelers, pilers, saw filers,
    skid greasers, slip tenders, teamsters, lumber shovers, tally-
    men, planers, bandsawmen, circular-saw-men, hoopers,
    matchers, nailers, painters, truckmen, packers, haulers,
For the sake of a tub or a pail to you.

And for the sake of a jack-knife in your pocket,
    or a scissors on your table,
The dynamite works get into production and deliver to the
    miners who blast, the mule drivers, engineers and firemen
    on the dinkies, the pumpmen, the rope riders, the sinkers
    and sorters, the carpenters, electricians and repairmen, the
    foremen and straw-bosses,
They get out the ore and send it to the smelters, the converters
    where by the hands and craft of furnace crushers and hot
    blast handlers, ladlers, puddlers, the drag-out man, the hook-
    up man, the chipper, the spannerman, the shearsman, the
    squeezer,
There is steel for the molders, the cutlers, buffers, finishers,
    forgers, grinders, polishers, temperers—
This for the sake of a jack-knife to your pocket or a shears on
    your table.
These are the people, with flaws and failings, with patience, sacri-
    fice, devotion, the people.

The people is a farmer, a tenant and a share-cropper, a plowman, a plow-grinder and a choreman, a churner, a chicken-picker and a combine driver, a threshing crew and an old settlers' picnic, a creamery co-operative, or a line of men on wagons selling tomatoes or sugar-beets on contract to a cannery, a refinery,

The people is a tall freight-handler and a tough longshoreman, a greasy fireman and a gambling oil-well shooter with a driller and tooler ready, a groping miner going underground with a headlamp, an engineer and a fireman with an eye for sema-phores, a seaman, deckhand, pilot at the wheel in fog and stars.

The people? A weaver of steel-and-concrete floors and walls fifty floors up, a blue-print designer, an expert calculator and accountant, a carpenter with an eye for joists and elbows, a bricklayer with an ear for the pling of a trowel, a pile-driver crew pounding down the pier-posts.

The people? Harness bulls and narcotic dicks, multigraph girls and soda-jerkers, hat girls, bat boys, sports writers, ghost writers, popcorn and peanut squads, flatfeet, scavengers, mugs saying "Aw go button your nose," squirts hollering "Aw go kiss yourself outa dis game intuh anuddah," dead-heads, hops, cappers, come-ons, tin horns, small timers, the night club outfits helping the soup-and-fish who have to do something between midnight and bedtime.

The people? A puddler in the flaring splinters of newmade steel, a milk-wagon-driver getting the once-over from a milk in-spector, a sand-hog with "the bends," a pack-rat, a snow-queen, janitors, jockeys, white collar lads, pearl divers, ped-

dlers, bundlestiffs, pants pressers, cleaners and dyers, lice and
rat exterminators.

So many forgotten, so many never remembered at all, yet there
are well-diggers, school-teachers, window washers who unless buckled proper dance on air and go down down, coal
heavers, roundhouse wipers, hostlers, sweepers, samplers,
weighers, sackers, carvers, bloom chippers, kiln burners,
cooks, bakers, beekeepers, goat raiser, goat hay growers, slag-
rollers, melters, solderers, track greasers, jiggermen, snow-
plow drivers, clamdiggers, stoolpigeons, the buck private,
the gob, the leatherneck, the cop—

In uniform, in white collars, in overalls, in denim and gingham,
a number on an assembly line, a name on a polling list, a
postoffice address, a crime and sports page reader, a movie
goer and radio listener, a stock-market sucker, a sure thing
for slick gamblers, a union man or non-union, a job holder
or a job hunter,

Always either employed, disemployed, unemployed and employ-
able or unemployable, a world series fan, a home buyer on a
shoestring, a down-and-out or a game fighter who will die
fighting.

> The people is the grand canyon of humanity
>   and many many miles across.
> The people is pandora's box, humpty dumpty,
>   a clock of doom and an avalanche when it
>   turns loose.
> The people rest on land and weather, on time
>   and the changing winds.

The people have come far and can look back
    and say, "We will go farther yet."
The people is a plucked goose and a shorn
    sheep of legalized fraud
And the people is one of those mountain slopes
    holding a volcano of retribution,
Slow in all things, slow in its gathered wrath,
    slow in its onward heave,
Slow in its asking: "Where are we now? what time
    is it?"

98

Hold down the skylines now with your themes,
Proud marching oblongs of floodlighted walls.
Your bottom rocks and caissons rest
In money and dreams, in blood and wishes.

Stand on your tall haunches of checkered windows
    with your spikes of white light
Speaking across the cool blue of the night mist:
    Can we read our writing?
    What are we saying on the skyline?

Tell it to us, skyscrapers around Wacker Drive in Chicago,
Tall oblongs in orchestral confusion from Battery to Bronx,
Along Market Street to the Ferry flashing the Golden Gate
    sunset,
Steel-and-concrete witnesses gazing down in San Antonio on the
    little old Alamo,
Gazing down in Washington on the antiques of Pennsylvania
    Avenue: what are these so near my feet far down?
Blinking across old Quaker footpaths of the City of Brotherly
    Love: what have we here? shooting crossed lights on the old
    Boston Common: who goes there?
Rising in Duluth to flicker with windows over Lake Superior,
    standing up in Atlanta to face toward Kenesaw Mountain,
Tall with steel automotive roots in Detroit, with transport, coal
    and oil roots in Toledo, Cleveland, Buffalo, flickering afar
    to the ore barges on Lake Erie, to the looming chainstore
    trucks on the hard roads,
Wigwagging with air beacons on Los Angeles City hall, telling

the Mississippi traffic it's nighttime in St. Louis, New Orleans, Minneapolis and St. Paul—
Can we read our writing? what are we saying on the skyline?
Hold down your horizon spikes of light, proud marching oblongs.
Your bottom rocks and pilings rest in money and dreams, in blood and wishes.
The structural iron workers, the riveters and bolt catchers, know what you cost.

Yes, who are these on the harbor skyline,
With the sun gone down and the funnels and checkers of light talking?
Who are these tall witnesses? who these high phantoms?
What can they tell of a thousand years to come,
People and people rising and fading with the springs and autumns, people like leaves out of the earth in spring, like leaves down the autumn wind—
What shall a thousand years tell a young tumultuous restless people?
They have made these steel skeletons like themselves—
Lean, tumultuous, restless:

      They have put up tall witnesses,
      to fade in a cool midnight blue,
      to rise in evening rainbow prints.

99

The man in the street is fed
with lies in peace, gas in war,
and he may live now
just around the corner from you
trying to sell
the only thing he has to sell,
the power of his hand and brain
to labor for wages, for pay,
for cash of the realm.
And there are no takers, he can't connect.
Maybe he says, "Some pretty good men are on the street."
Maybe he says, "I'm just a palooka . . . all washed up."
Maybe he's a wild kid ready for his first stickup.
Maybe he's bummed a thousand miles and has a diploma.
Maybe he can take whatever the police can hand him,
Too many of him saying in their own wild way,
"The worst they can give you is lead in the guts."
Whatever the wild kids want to do they'll do
And whoever gives them ideas, faiths, slogans,
Whoever touches the bottom flares of them,
Connects with something prouder than all deaths
For they can live on hard corn and like it.
They are the original sons of the wild jackass
Crowned and clothed with what the Unknown Soldier had
If he went to his fate in a pride over all deaths.
Give them a cause and they are a living dynamite.
They are the game fighters who will die fighting.

Here and there a man in the street
is young, hard as nails,
cold with questions he asks
from his burning insides.
    Bred in a motorized world of trial and error
    He measures by millionths of an inch,
    Knows ball bearings from spiral gearings,
    Chain transmission, heat treatment of steel,
    Speeds and feeds of automatic screw machines,
    Having handled electric tools
    With pistol grip and trigger switch.
Yet he can't connect and he can name thousands
Like himself idle amid plants also idle.
He studies the matter of what is justice
And revises himself on money, comfort, good name.
He doesn't know what he wants
And says when he gets it he'll know it.
    He asks, "Why is this what it is?"
    He asks, "Who is paying for this propaganda?"
    He asks, "Who owns the earth and why?"
Here and there a wife or sweetheart sees with him
The pity of being sold down the river in a smoke
Of confusions taken from the mouths of the dead
And spoken as though those dead are alive now
And would say now what they said then.

"Let him go as far as he likes," says one lawyer who sits on
    several heavy directorates.
"What do we care? Is he any of our business? If he knew how
    he could manage.

"There are exceptional cases but where there is poverty you will
generally find they were improvident and lacking in thrift
and industry.

"The system of free competition we now have has made America
the greatest and richest country on the face of the globe.

"You will seek in vain for any land where so large a number
of people have had so many of the good things of life.

"The malcontents who stir up class feeling and engender class
hatred are the foremost enemies of our republic and its con-
stitutional government."

And so on and so on in further confusions taken from the mouths
of the dead and spoken as though those dead are alive now
and would say now what they said then.

> Like the form of a seen and unheard prowler,
> Like a slow and cruel violence,
> is the known unspoken menace:
> Do what we tell you or go hungry;
> listen to us or you don't eat.

> He walks and walks and walks
> and wonders why the hell he built the road.

> Once I built a railroad
> . . . now . . .
> brother, can you spare a dime?

> To his dry well a man carried
> all the water he could carry,
> primed the pump, drew out the water,

and now
he has all the water he can carry.

We asked the cyclone
to go around our barn
but it didn't hear us.

100

The Great Sphinx and the Pyramids say:
"Man passed this way and saw
  a lot of ignorant besotted pharaohs."
The pink pagodas, jade rams and marble elephants
    of China say:
"Man came along here too
  and met suave and cruel mandarins."
The temples and forums of Greece and Rome say:
"Man owned man here where man bought and sold
    man in the open slave auctions; by these chat-
    tels stone was piled on stone to make these now
    crumbled pavilions."
The medieval Gothic cathedrals allege:
"Mankind said prayers here for itself and for stiff-
    necked drunken robber barons."
And the skyscrapers of Manhattan, Detroit, Chi-
    cago, London, Paris, Berlin—what will they
    say when the hoarse and roaring years of
    their origin have sunk to a soft whispering?

Will the same fathoms come for the skyscrapers?
Will the years heave and the wind and rain haul
    and hover
Till sand and dust have picked the locks and blown
    the safes and smashed the windows and filled
    the elevator-shafts and packed the rooms and
    made ashes of the papers, the stocks and bonds,
    the embossed and attested securities?

Will it be colder and colder yet with ice on the
ashes?

Even though the title-deeds read "forever and in
perpetuity unto heirs and assigns for all time
this deed is executed"?

Will it be all smoothed over into a hush where no
one pleads

"Who were they? where did they come from? and
why were they in such a hurry when they
knew so little where they were going?"

As between the rulers and the ruled-over what
does the record say?

Name the empires and republics with rulers wise
beyond their people.

When have they read the signs and recognized a
bridge generation?

When have the overlords and their paid liars and
strumpets

Held as a first question, "What do the people want
besides what we tell them they ought for their
own good to want?"?

And second, "How much of living fact is under
these cries and revolts, these claims that ex-
ploiters ride the people?"?

And third, "What do they do to themselves who
sell out the people?"?

When hush money is paid
to whom does it go

and by whom is it paid
and why should there be a hush?

When aldermen and legislative members say,
"We can put this through for you but it will take a
   little grease,"
What is the grease they mean and from whom
   comes this grease?
Let this be spoken of softly. Let sleeping dogs lie.
   What you don't know won't hurt you.
The trail leads straight to those in the possession of
   grease, the big shots of bespoken and anointed
   interests.

When violence is hired
and murder is paid for
and tear gas, clubs, automatics,
and blam blam machine guns
join in the hoarse mandate,
"Get the hell out of here,"
why then reserve a Sabbath
and call it a holiness day
for the mention of Jesus Christ
and why drag in the old quote,
"Thou shalt love thy neighbor
      as thyself"?

Said a lady wearing orchids
for a finality they betoken
distinct from cabbages
aloof from potatoes

and speaking with a white finality
from a face molded in half-secrets:
"Some things go unspoken in our circle:
no one has the bad grace to bring them up:
they exist and they don't:
when you belong you don't mention them."

Between highballs at the club amid the commodious leather
chairs, only the souse, the fool, would lift a glass with the
toast:
"Here's to the poor! let 'em suffer, they're used to it."
And if a boy fresh from college and the classics offers the point,
"Money sometimes rots people,"
He'll hear from someone: "Maybe so but you can't have too big
a surplus to take care of the future."

"There are men who can be hired
for work that must be done
and I would rather hire them
than do the work myself."
Thus in the front office
the big fellow in charge,
hired by absentee owners,
hired for work that must be done,
has an alibi and good reasons:
unless he keeps out of the red
he too goes: he hires and fires:
he is the overseer: in his ears
one droning iron murmur:
"We want results, re-sults.

"You'll show results or else."
So he hires and fires:
new names go on the payroll,
old names are dropped:
personnel, production, outlet, sales,
each has its own heebie-jeebies,
each brings its special jitters:
the picture always changes:
one little innocent new idea
one harmless looking patent
can wreck the works, the payrolls,
the mahogany front office,
the absentee owners:
unless the competitor is watched
and met and handled,
either killed off or satisfied,
the works go to rust,
to the weavers of cobwebs
weaving in iron and mahogany:
Thus in the front office amid the desk buttons
and the switchboard phone and the private line,
amid slips holding safe-combination-numbers,
amid the keys to safe-deposit-vaults
and the documents known to associates and attorneys
besides other documents held in reserve,
written communications private and confidential,
spoken messages not to be put in writing,
memoranda in low tone to Jones for immediate attention
and withheld from Abernathy for definite reasons
Abernathy having plenty enough to do as it is,

items touching rivals real and potential,
competitors ruthless with a jungle cunning,
competitors fighting in the open with a decent code,
competitors in the red and dazed by the graph
of volume and sales sliding down always down,
telegrams to be sent in cipher strictly and see to it,
telegrams for the press, for Congress, for the public,
quarterly earnings report for investors,
fully detailed report for the Chairman of the Board,
information sheets to be scanned and torn up,
other notations to be read closely and filed
in a fireproof private vault with a time-lock,
signed agreements hardly worth the public eye,
schedules, rebates, allowances working arrangements—
    amid these props
    of time and circumstance
    a big shot executive sits
with an eye on the board of directors first of all,
next the stockholders owning control,
next the vast eggheaded investing public,
and after these the men who run the works
from the engineers, chemists, geologists, intelligentsia
on to the white collar clerks and bookkeepers
and the overall crews who take whatever weather comes,
    in fumes and dust, in smoke, slag and cinders
    meeting production and delivery demands—
and finally the buyers, the consumers, the customers,
the people, yes, what will we let them have?
        Around a big table—decisions—
        wages up, wages down, wages as is—

             prices up, prices down, prices as is—
             this is the room and the big table
             of the high decisions.
They may consider lower prices
for the benefit of the consumer
or again to wreck a competitor.
They may hold prices down
because it's worth something to have
the good-will of the public, the mass buyers.
Or they may raise prices and get all they can
while the getting is good, explaining,
"We are not in business for our health,
  what we lose or win is *our* business."
Some of them trail with Marshall Field:
"The customer is always right," others with
Cornelius Vanderbilt: "The public be damned."
Others say one thing and do another.
And what have we here? what is this huddle?
Shall we call them scabs on their class?
Or are they talking to hear themselves talk?
They say Yes to Ford, to Filene, to Johnson,
to the Brookings Institution: one little idea:
After allowing for items to protect future operation
every cut in production cost should be shared
with the consumers in lower prices
with the workers in higher wages
thus stabilizing buying power
and guarding against recurrent collapses.
"What is this? Is it economics, poetry or what?
"Do you think you can run my business?

                                    267

"Are you trying to fly the flag
   of Soviet Russia over my office?"
You're in a room now where you hear
anything you want to hear
and the advice often runs:
        You can do anything you want to
        unless they stop you.

Sometimes they fight among themselves
in a dog-eat-dog struggle
for control and domination,
sending an opponent to the Isles of Greece,
leaving him not even a shirt,
or letting him leap from a tenth-floor fire-escape.

    What is to be said
        of those rare and suave swine
who pay themselves a fat swag of higher salaries
in the same year they pay stockholders nothing,
cutting payrolls in wage reductions and layoffs?

    What of those payday patriots
who took three hundred millions of profit dollars
        from powder and supply contracts
        in the same years other men by thousands
died with valor or took red wounds in a gray rain
        for the sake of a country, a flag?

Lincoln had a word for one crew: "respectable scoundrels."
They reaped their profits from the government's necessity in
money, blankets, guns, contracts,

And when they gambled on defeat in May of '64 and sent gold
     prices to new peaks
Lincoln groaned, "I wish every one of them had his devilish head
     shot off."

> One by one they will pass
> and be laid in numbered graves,
> one by one lights out
> and candles of remembrance
> and rest amid silver handles and heavy roses
> and forgotten hymns sung to their forgotten names.

101

The unemployed
without a stake in the country
without jobs or nest eggs
marching they don't know where
marching north south west—
and the deserts
marching east with dust
deserts out of howling dust-bowls
deserts with winds moving them
marching toward Omaha toward Tulsa—
these lead to no easy pleasant conversation
they fall into a dusty disordered poetry

"What was good for our fathers is good enough
for us—let us hold to the past and keep it
all and change it as little as we have to."
Since when has this been a counsel and light
of pioneers? of discoverers? of inventors?
of builders? of makers?

Who should be saying,
"We can buy anything, we always have,
we can fix anything, we always have,
we're not in the habit of losing,
on the main points we have our way,
we always have"?
who should be saying that and why?

As though yesterday is here today
and tomorrow too will be yesterday

and change on change is never hammered
on the deep anvils of transition
the words may be heard:
"Every so often these sons of the wild jackass
have to be handled. Let them come.
We've got the arguments, the propaganda machinery,
the money and the guns. Let them come.
What was good for our fathers is good enough for
us. We fight with the founding fathers."

What is the story of the railroads and banks,
of oil, steel, copper, aluminum, tin?
of the utilities of light, heat, power, transport?
what are the balances of pride and shame?
who took hold of the wilderness and changed it?
who paid the cost in blood and struggle?
what will the grave and considerate historian
loving humanity and hating no one dead or alive
have to write of wolves and people?
what are the names to be remembered with thanks?

Now they justify themselves to themselves:
we took things as we found them:
we never tried to shoot the moon:
we never pretended to be angels:
industry and science are slowly
making the world a better place to live in:
the weak must go under before the strong:
we'll always have the poor and the incompetent.

What then of those odd numbers
who have pretended to be angels

while using the fangs of wolves?
and what of the strong ones
who sat high and handsome
till they met stronger ones
till they were torn asunder
and outwolfed by bigger wolves?

And who plucked marvels
of industry and science
out of unexpected corners
unless it was the moon shooters
taking their chances
out in the great sky of the unknown?
who but they have held to a hope
poverty and the poor shall go
and the struggle of man for possessions
of music and craft and personal worth
lifted above the hog-trough level
above the animal dictate:
                    "Do this or go hungry"?

102

"Accordingly, they commenced by an insidious
debauching of the public mind . . . they have
been drugging the public mind."
What was this debauchery? what this drugging?
and how did Abraham Lincoln mean it July 4, 1861?
> The public *has* a mind?
> Yes.
> And men can follow a method
> and a calculated procedure
> for drugging and debauching it?
> Yes.
> And the whirlwind comes later?
> Yes.

Can you bewilder men by the millions
with transfusions of your own passions,
mixed with lies and half-lies,
texts torn from contexts,
and then look for peace, quiet, good-will
between nation and nation, race and race,
between class and class?

Who are these so ready
with a hate they are sure of,
with a prepared and considered hate?
who are these forehanded ones?

> Before the boys in blue and gray
> took the filth and gangrene

along with the glory,
Little Aleck Stephens, hazel-eyed
and shrunken, saw it coming:
"When I am on one of two trains coming in
opposite directions on a single track,
both engines at high speed—and both
engineers drunk—I get off at the first
station."

Is there a time to counsel,
"Be sober and patient while yet saying Yes
to freedom for cockeyed liars and bigots"?
Is there a time to say,
"The facts and guide measurements are yet
to be found and put to work: there are
dawns and false dawns read in a ball of
revolving crystals"?
Is there a time to repeat,
"The living passion of millions can rise
into a whirlwind: the storm once loose
who can ride it? you? or you? or you?
only history, only tomorrow, knows
for every revolution breaks
as a child of its own convulsive hour
shooting patterns never told of beforehand"?

103

The wind in the corn leaves among the naked stalks
and the assurances of the October cornhuskers
throwing the yellow and gold ears into wagons
and the weatherworn boards of the oblong corncribs
and the heavy boots of winter roaring
around the barn doors
and the cows drowsing in peace at the feed-boxes—
while sheet steel is riveted into ships and bridges
and the hangar night shift meets the air mail
and the steam shovels scoop gravel by the ton
and the interstate trucks parade on the hard roads
and the bread line silhouettes stand in a drizzle
and in Iowa the state fair prize hog crunches corn
and on the truck farms this year's scarecrows
lose the clothes they wore this summer
and stand next year in a change of rags—
these are chapters interwoven of the people.

When a slow dim light moves
on the face of vast waters
and in its slow dim changing
baffles keen old captains
the reading of the light
in its shifting resolves
is the same as trying to read
the hosts of circumstance
deepening the paths of action
with a decree for the people:

"Tomorrow you do this because
you can do nothing else."

What is it now
in the hosts of circumstance
where plainspoken men multiply,
what is it now the people are saying
near enough to the ribs of life
and the flowing face of vast waters
so they will go on saying it
in deepening paths of action
running toward a slow dim decree:
  "You do this because
    you can do nothing else"?

104

When was it long ago the murmurings began
and the joined murmurings
became a moving wall
moving with the authority of a great sea
whose Yes and No
stood in an awful script
in a new unheard-of handwriting?
"No longer," began the murmurings,
"shall the king be king
"nor the son of the king become king.
"Their authority shall go
"and their thrones be swept away.
"They are too far from us, the people.
"They listen too little to us, the people.
"They hold their counsels
"without men from the people given a word.
"Their ears are so far from us,
"so far from our wants and small belongings,
"we must trim the kings
"into something less than kings."
And the joined murmurings became a moving wall
with Yes and No in an awful script.
And the kings became less.
The kings shrank.

> What is it now
> the people are beginning
> to say—

is it this?
and if so
whither away and
where do we go
from here?
"What about the munitions and money kings,
the war lords and international bankers?
the transportation and credit kings?
the coal, the oil, and the mining kings?
the price-fixing monopoly control kings?
Why are they so far from us?
why do they hold their counsels
without men from the people given a word?
Shall we keep these kings and let their sons
in time become the same manner of kings?
Are their results equal to their authority?
Why are these interests too sacred for discussion?
What documents now call for holy daylight?
what costs, prices, values, are we forbidden to ask?
Are we slowly coming to understand
the distinction between a demagogue squawking
and the presentation of tragic plainspoken fact?
Shall a robber be named a robber when he is one
even though bespoken and anointed he is?
Shall a shame and a crime be mentioned
when it is so plainly there,
when day by day it draws toil, blood, and hunger,
enough of slow death and personal tragedy to certify
the kings who sit today as entrenched kings
are far too far from their people?

What does justice say?
or if justice is become an abstraction or a harlot
what does her harder sister, necessity, say?
Their ears are so far from us,
so far from our wants and small belongings
we must trim these kings of our time
into something less than kings.
Of these too it will be written:
    these kings shrank."
        What is it now
        the people are beginning
        to say—
        is it this?
        and if so
        whither away and
        where do we go from here?

105

Always the storm of propaganda blows.
Buy a paper. Read a book. Start the radio.
Listen in the railroad car, in.the bus,
Go to church, to a movie, to a saloon.
And always the breezes of personal opinion
are blowing mixed with the doctrines
of propaganda or the chatter of selling spiels.
Believe this, believe that. Buy these, buy them.
Love one-two-three, hate four-five-six.
Remember 7-8-9, forget 10-11-12.
Go now, don't wait, go now at once and buy
Dada Salts Incorporated, Crazy Horse Crystals,
for whatever ails you and if nothing ails you
it is good for that and we are telling you
for your own good. Whatever you are told,
you are told it is for your own good and not
for the special interest of those telling you.
Planned economy is forethought and care.
Planned economy is regimentation and tyranny.
What do you know about planned economy
and how did this argument get started and why?
Let the argument go on.

The storm of propaganda blows always.
In every air of today the germs float and hover.
The shock and contact of ideas goes on.
Planned economy will arrive, stand up,
and stay a long time—or planned economy will
take a beating and be smothered.

The people have the say-so.
Let the argument go on.
Let the people listen.
Tomorrow the people say Yes or No by one question:
    "What else can be done?"
In the drive of faiths on the wind today the people know:
"We have come far and we are going farther yet."

Who was the quiet silver-toned agitator who
said he loved every stone of the streets of
Boston, who was a believer in sidewalks, and
had it, "The talk of the sidewalk today is
the law of the land tomorrow"?

"The people," said a farmer's wife in a Minnesota country store
    while her husband was buying a new post-hole digger,
"The people," she went on, "will stick around a long time.
"The people run the works, only they don't know it yet—you
    wait and see."

    Who knows the answers, the cold inviolable truth?
And when have the paid and professional liars done else than
    bring wrath and fire, wreck and doom?
And how few they are who search and hesitate and say:
"I stand in this whirlpool and tell you I don't know and if I did
    know I would tell you and all I am doing now is to guess
    and I give you my guess for what it is worth as one man's
    guess.
"Yet I have worked out this guess for myself as nobody's yes-man
    and when it happens I no longer own the priceless little piece

of territory under my own hat, so far gone that I can't even do my own guessing for myself,

"Then I will know I am one of the unburied dead, one of the moving walking stalking talking unburied dead."

106

Sleep is a suspension midway
and a conundrum of shadows
lost in meadows of the moon.
  The people sleep.
    Ai! ai! the people sleep.
Yet the sleepers toss in sleep
and an end comes of sleep
and the sleepers wake.
    Ai! ai! the sleepers wake!

107

The people will live on.
The learning and blundering people will live on.
They will be tricked and sold and again sold
And go back to the nourishing earth for rootholds,
The people so peculiar in renewal and comeback,
You can't laugh off their capacity to take it.
The mammoth rests between his cyclonic dramas.

The people so often sleepy, weary, enigmatic,
is a vast huddle with many units saying:
"I earn my living.
I make enough to get by
and it takes all my time.
If I had more time
I could do more for myself
and maybe for others.
I could read and study
and talk things over
and find out about things.
It takes time.
I wish I had the time."

The people is a tragic and comic two-face:
hero and hoodlum: phantom and gorilla twist-
ing to moan with a gargoyle mouth: "They
buy me and sell me . . . it's a game . . .
sometime I'll break loose . . ."

Once having marched
Over the margins of animal necessity,
Over the grim line of sheer subsistence
    Then man came
To the deeper rituals of his bones,
To the lights lighter than any bones,
To the time for thinking things over,
To the dance, the song, the story,
Or the hours given over to dreaming,
    Once having so marched.

Between the finite limitations of the five senses
and the endless yearnings of man for the beyond
the people hold to the humdrum bidding of work and food
while reaching out when it comes their way
for lights beyond the prison of the five senses,
for keepsakes lasting beyond any hunger or death.
    This reaching is alive.
The panderers and liars have violated and smutted it.
    Yet this reaching is alive yet
    for lights and keepsakes.

      The people know the salt of the sea
      and the strength of the winds
      lashing the corners of the earth.
      The people take the earth
      as a tomb of rest and a cradle of hope.
      Who else speaks for the Family of Man?
      They are in tune and step
      with constellations of universal law.

The people is a polychrome,
a spectrum and a prism
held in a moving monolith,
a console organ of changing themes,
a clavilux of color poems
wherein the sea offers fog
and the fog moves off in rain
and the labrador sunset shortens
to a nocturne of clear stars
serene over the shot spray
of northern lights.

The steel mill sky is alive.
The fire breaks white and zigzag
shot on a gun-metal gloaming.
Man is a long time coming.
Man will yet win.
Brother may yet line up with brother:

This old anvil laughs at many broken hammers.
There are men who can't be bought.
The fireborn are at home in fire.
The stars make no noise.
You can't hinder the wind from blowing.
Time is a great teacher.
Who can live without hope?

In the darkness with a great bundle of grief
the people march.
In the night, and overhead a shovel of stars for
keeps, the people march:
                              "Where to? what next?"

DATE DUE

PRINTED IN U.S.A.